THEORY TEST for MOTORCYCLISTS

All the recommended revision questions and answers for motorcyclists from the DVSA

Published by AA Publishing (a trading name of AA Media Limited, whose registered office is Fanum House, Basing View, Basingstoke, Hampshire RG21 4EA; registered number 06112600).

© AA Media Limited 2018
Fourth edition

ISBN: 978-0-7495-7997-5

theAA.com

Printed in Dubai by Oriental Press Ltd

Cover images: © fckncg/Alamy Stock Photo

A05639

Contents

Getting your licence

The following three things will help you achieve your goal – getting your licence.

- Acquire knowledge of the rules through your instructor and by studying *The Highway Code*.
- Take the right attitude. Be careful, courteous and considerate to all other road users.
- Learn and understand the skills of riding a motorcycle by taking lessons from a fully qualified motorcycle instructor.

This book can help you become a careful and safe motorcycle rider and take the first step towards achieving your goal – preparing for your theory test.

Six essential steps to getting your motorcycle licence

If you already hold a car driving licence, or are upgrading an existing motorcycle licence to a higher category, the steps to getting a motorcycle licence will be different from those given below and you may not need to go through all the stages. The following steps apply to all new learner riders. See the motoring section of gov.uk for further advice.

1 Get your provisional licence

You can apply for a provisional licence from the age of 15 years and 9 months. To legally begin learning to ride, at the appropriate date, you must be in possession of a photocard provisional licence.

To apply online you must:

- be a UK resident (there's a different process for residents of Northern Ireland)
- meet the minimum age requirement

- have a valid debit or credit card
- meet the minimum eyesight requirement
- not be prevented from driving for any reason
- have your National Insurance number
- have a valid UK passport
- provide previous addresses for the last 3 years

To apply for a provisional licence:

Online: gov.uk/apply-first-provisional-driving-licence (in Northern Ireland use nidirect.gov.uk/articles/apply-provisional-driving-licence)
Tel: 0300 790 6801
Textphone: 0300 123 1278
Lines are open Monday to Friday, 8am to 7pm and Saturday, 8am to 2pm

You can also apply by post using application form D1 available from the Post Office or the Driver and Vehicle Licensing Agency (DVLA) online ordering service: gov.uk/dvlaforms. Send your application form and payment to DVLA, Swansea, SA99 1AD.

Residents of Northern Ireland or outside the UK must apply by post (see nidirect.gov.uk/articles/apply-provisional-driving-licence for an up-to-date list of required documents and the full process).

2 Learn *The Highway Code*

The Highway Code is essential reading for all road users, not just those learning to ride. It sets out all the rules for safe motorcycle riding, as well as the rules for other road users such as car drivers and pedestrians. When you have learned the rules you will be able to answer most of the questions in the theory test.

How many tests?

There are several stages for learner motorcyclists to complete:

- Compulsory Basic Training (CBT),
- Theory test (multiple-choice questions and hazard perception)
- Practical test Module 1 – Off Road
- Practical test Module 2 – On Road

You must pass the CBT and theory test before you are allowed to apply for the practical tests.

The government may change elements of the tests from time to time – ask your instructor or check gov.uk for any recent changes.

3 Take the theory test

The theory test has two parts

- multiple choice questions
- hazard perception clips

Both are taken, one after the other, on the same day.

You can book your test online or by phone if you have special requirements at the test. You can take a theory test in English or Welsh. It is possible to have a voice over if you have dyslexia or other reading difficulty.

To book your test:
Online: gov.uk/book-theory-test
Tel: 0300 200 11 22
Textphone: 0300 200 11 66
Lines are open Monday to Friday, 8am to 4pm

At the test centre you'll need your provisional photocard licence. If you have an old-style paper licence, you must take your signed driving licence and a valid passport. No other form of photographic identification will be accepted.

4 Compulsory Basic Training (CBT)

Most learner motorcycle and moped riders must take Compulsory Basic Training (CBT). Your CBT must also be taken with an approved training body (ATB). To find an ATB or for more information about CBT exemption visit gov.uk/find-motorcycle-training.

CBT is a training course that includes classroom and riding skills. The CBT, once completed, provides the rider with a certificate (DL196). This is valid for two years and in conjunction with the provisional motorcycle licence entitles the rider to ride a moped or a motorbike up to 125cc and with a power output of up to 11kW on the road.

You must use L plates (L or D plates in Wales) until you pass your full motorcycle test. The rider, however, cannot carry a pillion passenger or use motorways.

See gov.uk/motorcycle-cbt for further details.

5 Take the practical test

Once you've passed CBT and the theory test you can, with your instructor's guidance, plan ahead for a suitable test date for Modules 1 and 2 of the practical test.

The majority of motorcycle riders learn the necessary riding skills quite quickly and most training courses are between 3 to 5 days, depending on the rider's ability. Ensure the full official syllabus is covered and, as your skills develop, get as much practice as possible. Visit gov.uk/motorcycle-test/motorcycles-mopeds-you-can-use for the

Introduction

minimum test vehicle requirements to make sure that you take your practical test [Modules 1 and 2] on the size of motorcycle that you intend to ride.

To book your test:
Online: gov.uk/book-driving-test
Tel: 0300 200 11 22 if you have special requirements. Lines are open Monday to Friday 8am–12pm

Make sure you have the following details to hand when booking your practical test:

- theory test pass certificate number
- driver number shown on your licence
- your preferred date
- unacceptable days or periods when you can't make the test
- if you can accept a test at short notice
- disability or any special circumstances
- your credit/debit card details.

6 Apply for your full driving licence

After you've passed your practical test your examiner will send your provisional or driving licence and test certificate to the DVLA and you will receive your licence by post within three weeks of passing Module 2 of your practical test. When you receive your licence, it is important that you check that the correct motorcycle category has been added on the reverse of your photocard licence.

Once you have taken and passed your practical test, you will receive a licence, depending on your age and the size of motorcycle that you used for your practical test (Modules 1 and 2) – see opposite.

MOPED LICENCE CATEGORIES
AM: Two- or three-wheeled vehicles mopeds with maximum design speed of over 25km/h (15.5mph) but not more than 45km/h (28mph). Also includes light quad bikes.

P: Two-wheeled vehicles with a maximum design speed of over 45km/h (28mph) but not more than 50km/h (31mph) and an engine size of no more than 50cc if powered by an internal combustion engine.

Q: Two-wheeled vehicles with a maximum design speed of no more than 25km/h (15.5mph) and an engine size of not more than 50cc.

MOTORCYCLES LICENCE CATEGORIES
A1: Light motorbikes with an engine size of 125cc, a power output of 11kW and a power to weight ratio of not more than 0.1kW/kg.

A2: Motorbikes with a power output of up to 35kW and a power to weight ratio not more than 0.2kW/kg.

A: Motorbikes with a power output more than 35kW or a power to weight ratio more than 0.2kW/kg.

Visit gov.uk/driving-licence-categories for full details.

About the
theory test

Revising for the theory test

The theory test is all about making you a safer rider and it is a good idea to prepare for the theory test at the same time as you develop your skills for the practical test. By preparing for both tests at the same time, you will reinforce your knowledge and understanding of all aspects of riding and improve your chances of passing your tests first time.

How to use this book

This book is designed to help you prepare for the multiple-choice questions part of the theory test and contains all the official revision questions from the Driver and Vehicle Standards Agency (DVSA). The theory test consists of 50 unseen theory test questions based on the topics in this book (see pages 16–209). The real test questions are not published, but you can use this book to help you revise for the test.

To help you study for the test, the questions are arranged into the theory test topics. Each topic has its own colour band to help you find your way through the book.

Start your revision by picking a topic; you don't have to study the topics in order. Study each question carefully to make sure you understand what it is asking you. Look carefully at any diagram or photograph before reading the explanatory information and deciding on your answer.

All the correct answers are given in the back of this book (see pages 217–222). You'll also find a short glossary near the back of this book (pages 210–216), which explains some of the more difficult words and terms used in the theory test.

Remember

- Learning *The Highway Code* and getting some on-road riding experience are the best way to prepare for your theory test.
- Don't attempt too many questions at once.
- Don't try to learn the questions and answers by heart; the real test questions are not available for you to practice and are different from the revision questions given in this book.

Questions marked **NI** are **not** found in theory tests in Northern Ireland.

1 Study the question carefully and make sure you understand what it is asking you.

212 Mark *one* answer
What's the main hazard the driver of the red car (arrowed) should be aware of?

3 Look carefully at any photograph, symbol or diagram given within the question.

☐ **A** Glare from the sun may affect the driver's vision
☐ **B** The black car may stop suddenly
☐ **C** The bus may move out into the road
☐ **D** Oncoming vehicles will assume the driver is turning right

2 Read through all the possible options.

If you can do so safely, give way to buses signalling to move off at bus stops. Try to anticipate the actions of other road users around you. The driver of the red car should be prepared for the bus pulling out. As you approach a bus stop, look to see how many passengers are waiting to board. If the last one has just got on, the bus is likely to move off.

4 Each question in this book is accompanied by an explanation that will help you understand the theory behind the question and what answer may be appropriate. Make sure you read through this text before answering the question. This text will not appear in your actual theory test.

What to expect in the theory test

The theory test consists of two parts: 50 multiple-choice questions and hazard perception. You have to pass both parts in order to pass your theory test. You will receive your test scores at the end of the test. Even if you only failed on one part of the theory test, you still have to take both parts again next time.

Multiple-choice questions

You will have 57 minutes to complete the question part of the test using a touch-screen and all the questions are multiple-choice. The 50 questions appear on the screen one at a time and you can return to any of the questions within the 57 minutes to re-check or change your answers. You have to score a minimum of 43 out of 50 to pass. The Government may change the pass mark from time to time. Your driving school or the DVSA will be able to tell you if there has been a change.

Each question has four possible options. You must select the one correct answer. Don't worry about accidentally missing marking an answer because you'll be reminded that you haven't chosen an answer before moving on to the next question.

Study each question thoroughly and look carefully at any diagram, drawing or photograph. Before you look at the options given, decide what you think the correct answer might be. Read through the options and then select the answer that matches the one you had decided on. If you follow this system, you will avoid being confused by answers that appear to be similar.

You can answer the questions in any order you choose by moving forwards and backwards through the questions. You can also change your answer if necessary and flag questions you're unsure about, then go back to them later in the test. Your remaining time is shown on the screen.

Case study questions

Typically, five of the 50 questions will take the form of a case study. All five questions will be based on a single driving situation and appear one at time.

Case studies are designed to test that you not only know your car theory but also that you understand how to apply your knowledge when faced with a given driving situation.

The case study in your theory test could be based on any driving scenario and ask questions from a range of topics in the DVSA's database of questions.

The sample case study on the following pages demonstrates how the case study questions may appear in your live test, so you'll know what to expect.

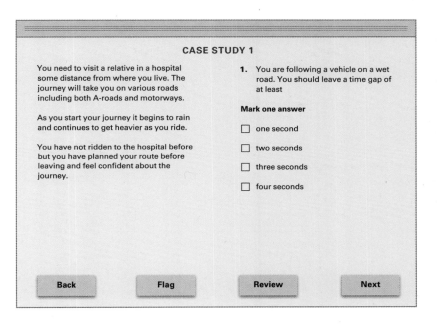

CASE STUDY 1

You need to visit a relative in a hospital some distance from where you live. The journey will take you on various roads including both A-roads and motorways.

As you start your journey it begins to rain and continues to get heavier as you ride.

You have not ridden to the hospital before but you have planned your route before leaving and feel confident about the journey.

1. You are following a vehicle on a wet road. You should leave a time gap of at least

Mark one answer

☐ one second

☐ two seconds

☐ three seconds

☐ four seconds

Back   Flag   Review   Next

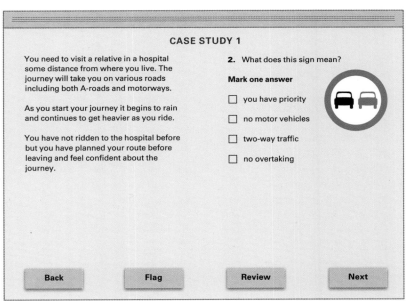

CASE STUDY 1

You need to visit a relative in a hospital some distance from where you live. The journey will take you on various roads including both A-roads and motorways.

As you start your journey it begins to rain and continues to get heavier as you ride.

You have not ridden to the hospital before but you have planned your route before leaving and feel confident about the journey.

2. What does this sign mean?

Mark one answer

☐ you have priority

☐ no motor vehicles

☐ two-way traffic

☐ no overtaking

Back   Flag   Review   Next

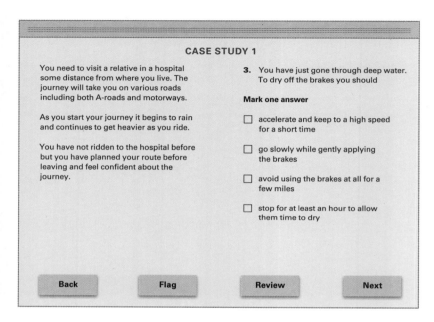

CASE STUDY 1

You need to visit a relative in a hospital some distance from where you live. The journey will take you on various roads including both A-roads and motorways.

As you start your journey it begins to rain and continues to get heavier as you ride.

You have not ridden to the hospital before but you have planned your route before leaving and feel confident about the journey.

3. You have just gone through deep water. To dry off the brakes you should

Mark one answer

☐ accelerate and keep to a high speed for a short time

☐ go slowly while gently applying the brakes

☐ avoid using the brakes at all for a few miles

☐ stop for at least an hour to allow them time to dry

| Back | Flag | Review | Next |

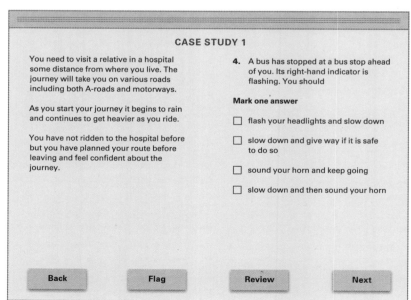

CASE STUDY 1

You need to visit a relative in a hospital some distance from where you live. The journey will take you on various roads including both A-roads and motorways.

As you start your journey it begins to rain and continues to get heavier as you ride.

You have not ridden to the hospital before but you have planned your route before leaving and feel confident about the journey.

4. A bus has stopped at a bus stop ahead of you. Its right-hand indicator is flashing. You should

Mark one answer

☐ flash your headlights and slow down

☐ slow down and give way if it is safe to do so

☐ sound your horn and keep going

☐ slow down and then sound your horn

| Back | Flag | Review | Next |

CASE STUDY 1

You need to visit a relative in a hospital some distance from where you live. The journey will take you on various roads including both A-roads and motorways.

As you start your journey it begins to rain and continues to get heavier as you ride.

You have not ridden to the hospital before but you have planned your route before leaving and feel confident about the journey.

5. Where you see street lights but no speed limit signs the limit is usually

Mark one answer

☐ 30mph

☐ 40mph

☐ 50mph

☐ 60mph

Back	Flag	Review	Next

Answers to sample case study questions: 1 D 2 D 3 B 4 B 5 A

Hazard perception

The video clip element of the theory test is known as hazard perception. Its aim is to find out how good you are at noticing potential problems developing on the road ahead. The test will also show how much you know about the risks to you as a rider and the risks to other road users.

Your driving instructor can help you learn hazard perception skills and can give you plenty of practice in what to look out for when riding, how to anticipate hazards, and what action to take to deal with hazards of all kinds.

What is a hazard?

A hazard is anything that might cause you to change speed or direction when riding. The hazard perception element of the theory test is about spotting developing hazards. This is one of the key skills of good riding and is also called anticipation. Anticipating hazards, such as car doors opening or children running into the road, means looking out for them in advance and taking the appropriate action.

As you get more driving experience you will start to learn about the times and places where you are most likely to meet hazards. An example of this is the rush hour. You know people take more risks when they are in a hurry. Maybe they have to drop their children at school before going to work. Perhaps they are late for a meeting or want to get home. You have to be prepared for bad driving – for example, another road user pulling out in front of you.

You won't be able to practise with the real clips used in the official test, of course, but practice software is widely available.

What to expect in the hazard perception test

After answering the multiple-choice questions, you will be given a short break before you begin the hazard perception part of the test. The hazard perception test lasts for about 20 minutes. Before you start you will be given some instructions explaining how the test works; you'll also get a chance to practise with the computer and mouse before you start. This is to make sure that you know what to expect on the test and that you are happy with what you have to do.

Next you will see 14 clips of street scenes with traffic such as cars, cyclists, pedestrians etc. The scenes are from the point of view of a rider. You have to notice potential hazards that are developing on the road ahead – that is, problems that could lead to an incident. As soon as you notice a hazard developing, click the mouse. You will have plenty of time to see the hazard – the sooner you notice it, the more marks you score.

Each clip has at least one hazard in it but one clip has two – there are 15 hazard to spot in all. You have to score a minimum of 44 out of 75 to pass, but the pass mark may change so check with your instructor or the DVSA before sitting your test.

Note that the computer has checks built in to show anyone trying to cheat – for example someone who keeps clicking the mouse all the time. Be aware that, unlike the theory test questions, you will not have an opportunity to go back to an earlier clip and change your response, so you need to concentrate throughout the test.

Further information

For more practical information on learning to ride visit www.gov.uk/browse/driving.

You responded to this clip
in an unacceptable manner.
You will score zero
for this clip.

Top: Click the mouse when you spot potential hazards – the tractor emerging from the side road (ringed in red).
Above: You may see a warning screen similar to this one if the computer detects a clicking pattern or you click. the mouse constantly.

Theory test revision questions

Contents   Page

1 Mark *one* answer

You're about to turn right. What should you do just before you turn?

- ☐ **A** Give the correct signal
- ☐ **B** Take a lifesaver glance over your shoulder
- ☐ **C** Select the correct gear
- ☐ **D** Get in position ready for the turn

When you're turning right, plan your approach to the junction. Signal and select the correct gear in good time. Just before you turn, take a lifesaver glance for a final check behind and to the side of you.

2 Mark *one* answer

What is the 'lifesaver' when riding a motorcycle?

- ☐ **A** A certificate every motorcyclist must have
- ☐ **B** A final rearward glance before changing direction
- ☐ **C** A part of the motorcycle tool kit
- ☐ **D** A mirror fitted to check blind spots

This action makes you aware of what's happening behind and alongside you. The lifesaver glance should be timed so that you still have time to react if it isn't safe to perform the manoeuvre.

3 Mark *one* answer

You see road signs showing a sharp bend ahead. What should you do?

- ☐ **A** Continue at the same speed
- ☐ **B** Slow down as you go around the bend
- ☐ **C** Slow down as you come out of the bend
- ☐ **D** Slow down before the bend

Always look for any advance warning of hazards, such as road signs and hazard warning lines. Use this information to plan ahead and to help you avoid the need for late, harsh braking. Your motorcycle should be upright and moving in a straight line when you brake. This will help you keep maximum control when dealing with the hazard.

4 Mark *one* answer

You're riding at night and are dazzled by the headlights of an oncoming car. What should you do?

- ☐ **A** Slow down or stop
- ☐ **B** Close your eyes
- ☐ **C** Flash your headlights
- ☐ **D** Turn your head away

If you're dazzled by the headlights of an approaching vehicle, slow down or stop until your eyes have adjusted. A dirty or scratched visor could make the dazzle worse and further impair your vision.

5 Mark *one* answer

When riding, your shoulders can obstruct the view in your mirrors. How can you overcome this?

- ☐ **A** Indicate earlier than normal
- ☐ **B** Fit smaller mirrors
- ☐ **C** Extend the mirror arms
- ☐ **D** Brake earlier than normal

It's essential that you have a clear view all around. Adjust your mirrors to give you the best view of the road behind. If your body obscures the view, try fitting mirrors with longer stems.

---

6 Mark *one* answer

When may motorcyclists use a mobile phone?

- ☐ **A** When they're carrying a pillion passenger
- ☐ **B** When they're parked in a safe place
- ☐ **C** When they're riding an automatic motorcycle
- ☐ **D** When they're riding on quiet roads

It's important that you're in full control at all times. Even using a hands-free phone kit can distract your attention from the road. If you need to use a mobile phone, stop in a safe and convenient place before making the call.

7 Mark *one* answer

You're riding at night. You have your headlights on main beam. Another vehicle is overtaking you. When should you dip your headlights?

- ☐ **A** When the other vehicle signals to overtake
- ☐ **B** As soon as the other vehicle moves out to overtake
- ☐ **C** As soon as the other vehicle passes you
- ☐ **D** After the other vehicle pulls in front of you

At night, you should dip your headlights to avoid dazzling oncoming drivers or those ahead of you. If you're being overtaken, dip your headlights as the other vehicle comes past. When you switch to dipped beam, your view of the road ahead will be reduced, so look ahead for hazards on your side of the road before you do so.

---

8 Mark *one* answer

How should you move off safely from a parked position?

- ☐ **A** Signal if other drivers will need to slow down
- ☐ **B** Leave your motorcycle on its stand until the road is clear
- ☐ **C** Give an arm signal as well as using your indicators
- ☐ **D** Look over your shoulder for a final check

Before you move off from the side of the road, you should take a final look over your shoulder to check your blind spot. This will help you to see any road user who isn't visible in your mirrors.

9 Mark *one* answer

You become cold when riding your motorcycle. How will this affect you?

☐ **A** You'll be more alert
☐ **B** You'll be more relaxed
☐ **C** You'll react more quickly
☐ **D** You'll lose concentration

It can be difficult to keep warm when riding a motorcycle. It's well worth buying good-quality motorcycle clothing, which will help to keep you warm and is essential for your safety. If you become very cold while riding, you'll find it difficult to concentrate on the road.

10 Mark *one* answer

You're riding at night and are dazzled by the lights of an approaching vehicle. What should you do?

☐ **A** Switch off your headlights
☐ **B** Switch to main beam
☐ **C** Slow down and stop if necessary
☐ **D** Flash your headlights

If your view of the road ahead is restricted because you're being dazzled by approaching headlights, slow down and, if you need to, pull over and stop.

11 Mark *one* answer

You should always check your blind spots before doing what?

☐ **A** Moving off
☐ **B** Slowing down
☐ **C** Changing gear
☐ **D** Giving a signal

Your blind spots are the areas behind and to either side of you that aren't covered by your mirrors. You should always check the relevant side when there's a risk of a hazard that isn't visible in your mirrors.

12 Mark *one* answer

Blind spots should be checked before you do what?

☐ **A** Give a signal
☐ **B** Apply the brakes
☐ **C** Change direction
☐ **D** Give an arm signal

The areas that aren't covered by your mirrors are called blind spots. They should always be checked before changing direction. This check is so important it's called the 'lifesaver'.

13 Mark *one* answer

When should you check the blind spots?

☐ **A** Before changing gear
☐ **B** Before giving signals
☐ **C** Before slowing down
☐ **D** Before changing lanes

The areas that aren't covered by your mirrors are called blind spots. Other vehicles may be hidden in these areas. Before changing lanes, you should make sure it's safe by checking the blind spot on the side you intend to move. This is called a lifesaver check.

14 Mark *one* answer

Why can it be helpful to have mirrors fitted on each side of your motorcycle?

☐ **A** To judge the gap when filtering in traffic
☐ **B** To give protection when riding in poor weather
☐ **C** To make your motorcycle appear larger to other drivers
☐ **D** To give you the best view of the road behind

When riding on the road, you need to know as much about following traffic as you can. A mirror fitted on each side of your motorcycle will help give you the best view of the road behind.

15 Mark *one* answer

What does the term 'lifesaver' mean?

☐ **A** A final rearward glance
☐ **B** An approved safety helmet
☐ **C** A reflective jacket
☐ **D** The two-second rule

There are areas behind and to either side of you that aren't visible in your mirrors. These are known as blind spots. Just before turning or changing direction, you should look around to check that there's nothing hazardous in the blind spot. This check is known as a 'lifesaver'.

16 Mark *one* answer

You're about to emerge from a junction. Your pillion passenger tells you it's clear. When should you rely on their judgement?

☐ **A** Never; you should always look for yourself
☐ **B** When the roads are very busy
☐ **C** When the roads are very quiet
☐ **D** Only when they're a qualified rider

Your passenger may be inexperienced in judging traffic situations, may have a poor view or may not have seen a potential hazard. You're responsible for your own safety and that of your passenger. Always make your own checks to be sure it's safe to pull out.

17 Mark *one* answer

What must you do before stopping normally?

☐ **A** Put both feet down
☐ **B** Select first gear
☐ **C** Use your mirrors
☐ **D** Move into neutral

Check your mirrors before slowing down or stopping, as there could be vehicles close behind you. If necessary, turn and look behind before stopping.

18 Mark *one* answer

Why should you check over your shoulder before you change lanes in busy, moving traffic?

☐ **A** To avoid having to give a signal
☐ **B** Mirrors don't cover blind spots
☐ **C** So traffic ahead will make room for you
☐ **D** So your balance won't be affected

Before changing lanes, make sure there's a safe gap to move into. Looking over your shoulder allows you to check the area not covered by your mirrors, where a vehicle could be hidden from view. It also warns following drivers that you want to change lanes.

19 Mark *one* answer

You've been waiting for some time to make a right turn into a side road. What should you do just before you make the turn?

☐ **A** Move close to the kerb
☐ **B** Select a higher gear
☐ **C** Make a lifesaver check
☐ **D** Wave to the oncoming traffic

Remember your lifesaver glance before you start to turn. If you've been waiting for some time and a queue has built up behind you, a vehicle further back may try to overtake. In this situation, it's especially important to look out for other motorcycles, which may be approaching at speed.

20 Mark *one* answer

You're turning right onto a dual carriageway. What should you do before emerging?

☐ **A** Stop, and then select a very low gear
☐ **B** Position in the left gutter of the side road
☐ **C** Check the width of the central reservation
☐ **D** Check that there's enough room for vehicles behind you

Before emerging right onto a dual carriageway, make sure that the central reservation is wide enough to protect your vehicle. If it isn't, you should treat it as one road and check that it's clear in both directions before pulling out.

21 Mark *one* answer

What should you do when riding a motorcycle you've never ridden before?

☐ **A** Ask someone to ride with you for the first time
☐ **B** Just ride, as all the controls and switches are the same
☐ **C** Leave your gloves behind, so the switches can be operated more easily
☐ **D** Make sure you know where all the controls and switches are

While control layouts are generally similar, different makes and models have subtle differences in the position and operation of the switches. Before you ride any motorcycle, make sure you're familiar with the layout of all the controls and switches.

22   Mark *one* answer
You're turning right at a large roundabout. What should you do before you cross a lane to reach your exit?

☐ **A** Take a lifesaver glance over your right shoulder
☐ **B** Put on your right indicator
☐ **C** Take a lifesaver glance over your left shoulder
☐ **D** Cancel the left indicator

On busy roundabouts, traffic may be moving very quickly and changing lanes suddenly. You need to be aware of what's happening all around you. Before crossing lanes to the left, make sure you take a lifesaver glance to the left. This gives you time to react if it isn't safe to make the manoeuvre.

23   Mark *one* answer
You're positioned to turn right on a multi-lane roundabout. What should you do before moving to a lane on your left?

☐ **A** Take a lifesaver glance over your right shoulder
☐ **B** Cancel the left signal
☐ **C** Signal to the right
☐ **D** Take a lifesaver glance over your left shoulder

Before you change lane you need to know whether it's safe to do so. A lifesaver glance in the direction you want to move will allow you to check your mirrors' blind spots. Your life could depend on knowing where other vehicles are.

24   Mark *one* answer
You're turning right on a multi-lane roundabout. When should you take a lifesaver glance over your left shoulder?

☐ **A** After moving into the left-hand lane
☐ **B** After leaving the roundabout
☐ **C** Before signalling to the right
☐ **D** Before moving into the left-hand lane

The 'lifesaver' is essential to motorcyclists and does exactly what it says: it could save your life. Its purpose is to check the blind spot that isn't covered by your mirrors. Learn and understand how and when you should use it.

25   Mark *one* answer
You see an incident on the other side of the motorway. What should you do?

☐ **A** Leave the motorway at the next exit
☐ **B** Stop and cross the carriageway to help
☐ **C** Concentrate on what's happening ahead
☐ **D** Place a warning triangle in the road

Always concentrate on the road ahead. Try not to be distracted by an incident on the other side of the road. Many motorway collisions occur due to traffic slowing down because drivers are looking at something on the other side of the road.

26 Mark *one* answer
What should you do before making a U-turn?

☐ **A** Give an arm signal as well as using your indicators
☐ **B** Check signs to see that U-turns are permitted
☐ **C** Look over your shoulder for a final check
☐ **D** Select a higher gear than normal

If you have to make a U-turn, slow down and ensure that the road is clear in both directions. Make sure that the road is wide enough for you to carry out the manoeuvre safely.

27 Mark *one* answer
What should you do as you approach this bridge?

☐ **A** Move to the right
☐ **B** Slow down
☐ **C** Change gear
☐ **D** Keep to 30 mph

You should slow down and be cautious. The bridge is narrow and there may not be enough room for you to pass an oncoming vehicle at this point. Also, there's no footpath, so be aware of pedestrians in the road.

28 Mark *one* answer
In which of these situations should you avoid overtaking?

☐ **A** Just after a bend
☐ **B** In a one-way street
☐ **C** On a 30 mph road
☐ **D** Approaching a dip in the road

As you begin to think about overtaking, ask yourself whether it's really necessary. If you can't see well ahead, stay back and wait for a safer place to pull out.

29 Mark *one* answer
What does the curved arrow on the road mean?

☐ **A** Heavy vehicles should take the next road on the left to avoid a weight limit
☐ **B** The road ahead bends to the left
☐ **C** Overtaking traffic should move back to the left
☐ **D** The road ahead has a camber to the left

In this picture, the road marking shows that overtaking drivers or riders need to return to the left. These markings show the direction drivers must pass hatch markings or solid double white lines. They are also used to show the route that high vehicles should take under low arched bridge.

30 Mark *one* answer
Your mobile phone rings while you're travelling. What should you do?

☐ **A** Stop immediately
☐ **B** Answer it immediately
☐ **C** Ignore it
☐ **D** Pull up at the nearest kerb

It's illegal to use a hand-held mobile or similar device when driving or riding, except in a genuine emergency. The safest option is to switch off your mobile phone before you set off, and use a message service. If you've forgotten to switch your phone off and it rings, you should ignore it. When you've stopped in a safe place, you can see who called and return the call if necessary.

31 Mark *one* answer
Why are these yellow lines painted across the road?

☐ **A** To help you choose the correct lane
☐ **B** To help you keep the correct separation distance
☐ **C** To make you aware of your speed
☐ **D** To tell you the distance to the roundabout

These lines are often found on the approach to a roundabout or a dangerous junction. They give you extra warning to adjust your speed. Look well ahead and do this in good time.

32 Mark *one* answer
What should you do when you're approaching traffic lights that have been on green for some time?

☐ **A** Accelerate hard
☐ **B** Maintain your speed
☐ **C** Be ready to stop
☐ **D** Brake hard

The longer traffic lights have been on green, the sooner they'll change. Allow for this as you approach traffic lights that you know have been on green for a while. They're likely to change soon, so you should be prepared to stop.

33 Mark *one* answer
What should you do before stopping?

☐ **A** Sound the horn
☐ **B** Use the mirrors
☐ **C** Select a higher gear
☐ **D** Flash the headlights

Before pulling up, check the mirrors to see what's happening behind you. Also assess what's ahead and make sure you give the correct signal if it will help other road users.

34 Mark *one* answer

You're following a large vehicle. Why should you stay a safe distance behind it?

- ☐ **A** You'll be able to corner more quickly
- ☐ **B** You'll help the large vehicle to stop more easily
- ☐ **C** You'll allow the driver to see you in their mirrors
- ☐ **D** You'll keep out of the wind better

If you're following a large vehicle but are so close to it that you can't see its exterior mirrors, the driver won't be able to see you. Keeping well back will also allow you to see the road ahead by looking past on either side of the large vehicle.

35 Mark *one* answer

When you see a hazard ahead, you should use the mirrors. Why is this?

- ☐ **A** Because you'll need to accelerate out of danger
- ☐ **B** To assess how your actions will affect following traffic
- ☐ **C** Because you'll need to brake sharply to a stop
- ☐ **D** To check what's happening on the road ahead

You should be constantly scanning the road for clues about what's going to happen next. Check your mirrors regularly, particularly as soon as you spot a hazard. What's happening behind may affect your response to hazards ahead.

36 Mark *one* answer

You're waiting to turn right at the end of a road. Your view is obstructed by parked vehicles. What should you do?

- ☐ **A** Stop and then move forward slowly and carefully for a clear view
- ☐ **B** Move quickly to where you can see so you only block traffic from one direction
- ☐ **C** Wait for a pedestrian to let you know when it's safe for you to emerge
- ☐ **D** Turn your vehicle around immediately and find another junction to use

At junctions, your view is often restricted by buildings, trees or parked cars. You need to be able to see in order to judge a safe gap. Edge forward slowly and keep looking all the time. Don't cause other road users to change speed or direction as you emerge.

37 Mark *one* answer

You're riding towards a zebra crossing. Pedestrians are waiting to cross. What should you do?

- ☐ **A** Give way to the elderly and infirm only
- ☐ **B** Slow down and prepare to stop
- ☐ **C** Use your headlights to signal them to cross
- ☐ **D** Wave at them to cross the road

As you approach a zebra crossing, look out for people waiting to cross and be ready to stop. Some pedestrians may be a little slow to understand that it's safe to cross, so give them time. Be patient and don't rev your engine or surge forward before the crossing is clear.

38 Mark *one* answer

You're following a large vehicle travelling at 40 mph. Where should you position your motorcycle?

- ☐ **A** Close behind the vehicle, to make it easier to overtake
- ☐ **B** To the left of the road, to make it easier to be seen
- ☐ **C** Close to the vehicle, to keep out of the wind
- ☐ **D** Well back, so that you can see past the vehicle

You need to be able to see well down the road and be ready for any hazards. Staying too close to the vehicle will reduce your view of the road ahead and the driver of the vehicle in front may not be able to see you either. Without a safe separation gap, you don't have the time and space you need to react to any hazards.

39 Mark *one* answer

You're approaching two riders on horseback. What should you do?

- ☐ **A** Continue at your normal speed
- ☐ **B** Change down the gears quickly
- ☐ **C** Slow down and be ready to stop
- ☐ **D** Flash your headlights to warn them

Animals are easily frightened by moving motor vehicles. If you're approaching horses, keep your speed down and watch to see if the rider has any difficulty keeping control. Always be ready to stop if necessary. When it's safe to pass, give them plenty of room.

40 Mark *one* answer

You're approaching a red light at a puffin crossing. Pedestrians are on the crossing. When will your red light change?

- ☐ **A** When you start to edge forward onto the crossing
- ☐ **B** When the pedestrians have reached a safe position
- ☐ **C** When the pedestrians are clear of the front of your motorcycle
- ☐ **D** When a driver from the opposite direction reaches the crossing

An electronic device will automatically detect when the pedestrians have reached a safe position. Don't move forward until the green light shows and you've checked that it's safe to proceed.

41 Mark *one* answer

You're riding a motorcycle that has an engine of less than 50 cc. What should you do if you see a queue of traffic building up behind?

☐ **A** Keep well out to stop vehicles overtaking dangerously

☐ **B** Wave vehicles behind you to pass if you think they can overtake

☐ **C** Pull in when you can to let faster vehicles behind you overtake

☐ **D** Give a left signal when it's safe for vehicles to overtake you

Try not to hold up a queue of traffic. This might lead to other road users becoming impatient and attempting dangerous manoeuvres. If you're riding a slow-moving scooter or small motorcycle and a queue of traffic has built up behind you, look for a safe place to pull in so they can pass safely.

42 Mark *one* answer

When you're riding a motorcycle, what should your normal road position allow?

☐ **A** Other vehicles will be able to pass easily on your left

☐ **B** You'll keep within half a metre (1 foot 8 inches) of the kerb

☐ **C** Faster traffic will be able to overtake you easily

☐ **D** Drivers at junctions ahead will be able to see you approaching

Aim to ride in the middle of your lane. Avoid riding in the gutter or in the centre of the road, where you might

- obstruct overtaking traffic
- put yourself in danger from oncoming traffic
- encourage other traffic to overtake you on the left.

43 Mark *one* answer

Why are young motorcyclists more likely to be involved in crashes?

☐ **A** Because they're too cautious at junctions

☐ **B** Because they ride in the middle of lanes

☐ **C** Because they're inexperienced

☐ **D** Because they ride in groups

Overconfidence, lack of experience and poor judgement can cause a motorcyclist to make poor decisions, which can lead to a collision. It's just as important to make sure you have the right attitude and self-awareness as a rider as it is to develop skilful riding techniques.

44 Mark *one* answer

At a pelican crossing, what must you do when the amber light is flashing?

- ☐ **A** Stop and wait for the green light
- ☐ **B** Stop and wait for the red light
- ☐ **C** Give way to pedestrians waiting to cross
- ☐ **D** Give way to pedestrians already on the crossing

Pelican crossings are signal-controlled crossings operated by pedestrians. Push-button controls change the signals. Pelican crossings have no red-and-amber stage before green; instead, they have a flashing amber light. This means you must give way to pedestrians who are already on the crossing. If the crossing is clear, however, you can continue.

45 Mark *one* answer

Why should you never wave people across at pedestrian crossings?

- ☐ **A** Another vehicle may be coming
- ☐ **B** They may not be looking
- ☐ **C** It's safer for you to carry on
- ☐ **D** They may not be ready to cross

If people are waiting to use a pedestrian crossing, slow down and be prepared to stop. Don't wave them across the road, because another driver may not have seen them, may not have seen your signal, and may not be able to stop safely.

46 Mark *one* answer

What does 'tailgating' mean?

- ☐ **A** Using the rear door of a hatchback car
- ☐ **B** Reversing into a parking space
- ☐ **C** Following another vehicle too closely
- ☐ **D** Driving with rear fog lights on

'Tailgating' is the term used when a driver or rider follows the vehicle in front too closely. It's dangerous because it restricts their view of the road ahead and leaves no safety margin if the vehicle in front needs to slow down or stop suddenly. Tailgating is often the underlying cause of rear-end collisions or multiple pile-ups.

47 Mark *one* answer

Why is it unwise to follow this vehicle too closely?

- ☐ **A** Your brakes will overheat
- ☐ **B** Your view ahead will be increased
- ☐ **C** Your engine will overheat
- ☐ **D** Your view ahead will be reduced

Staying back will increase your view of the road ahead. This will help you to see any hazards that might occur and give you more time to react.

48 Mark *one* answer

What's the minimum time gap you should leave when following a vehicle on a wet road?

☐ **A** One second
☐ **B** Two seconds
☐ **C** Three seconds
☐ **D** Four seconds

Water will reduce your tyres' grip on the road. The safe separation gap of at least two seconds in dry conditions should be doubled, to at least four seconds, in wet weather.

49 Mark *one* answer

A long, heavily laden lorry is taking a long time to overtake you. What should you do?

☐ **A** Speed up
☐ **B** Slow down
☐ **C** Hold your speed
☐ **D** Change direction

A long lorry with a heavy load will need more time to pass you than a car, especially on an uphill stretch of road. Slow down and allow the lorry to pass.

50 Mark *one* answer

Which vehicle will use a blue flashing beacon?

☐ **A** Motorway maintenance
☐ **B** Bomb disposal
☐ **C** Snow plough
☐ **D** Breakdown recovery

Emergency vehicles use blue flashing lights. If you see or hear one, move out of its way as soon as it's safe and legal to do so.

51 Mark *one* answer

You're being followed by an ambulance showing flashing blue lights. What should you do?

☐ **A** Pull over as soon as it's safe to do so
☐ **B** Accelerate hard to get away from it
☐ **C** Maintain your speed and course
☐ **D** Brake harshly and stop well out into the road

Pull over in a place where the ambulance can pass safely. Check that there are no bollards or obstructions in the road that will prevent it from passing.

52 Mark *one* answer

What type of emergency vehicle is fitted with a green flashing beacon?

☐ **A** Fire engine
☐ **B** Road gritter
☐ **C** Ambulance
☐ **D** Doctor's car

A green flashing beacon on a vehicle means the driver or passenger is a doctor on an emergency call. Give way to them if it's safe to do so. Be aware that the vehicle may be travelling quickly or may stop in a hurry.

53 Mark *one* answer
Who should obey diamond-shaped traffic signs?

- ☐ **A** Tram drivers
- ☐ **B** Bus drivers
- ☐ **C** Lorry drivers
- ☐ **D** Taxi drivers

These signs apply only to tram drivers, but you should know their meaning so that you're aware of the priorities and are able to anticipate the actions of the driver.

54 Mark *one* answer
On a road where trams operate, which of these vehicles will be most at risk from the tram rails?

- ☐ **A** Cars
- ☐ **B** Cycles
- ☐ **C** Buses
- ☐ **D** Lorries

The narrow wheels of a bicycle can become stuck in the tram rails, causing the cyclist to stop suddenly, wobble or even lose balance altogether. The tram lines are also slippery, which could cause a cyclist to slide or fall off.

55 Mark *one* answer
What should you use your horn for?

- ☐ **A** To alert others to your presence
- ☐ **B** To allow you right of way
- ☐ **C** To greet other road users
- ☐ **D** To signal your annoyance

Your horn mustn't be used between 11.30 pm and 7 am in a built-up area or when you're stationary, unless a moving vehicle poses a danger. Its function is to alert other road users to your presence.

56 Mark *one* answer
You're in a one-way street and want to turn right. There are two lanes. Where should you position your vehicle?

- ☐ **A** In the right-hand lane
- ☐ **B** In the left-hand lane
- ☐ **C** In either lane, depending on the traffic
- ☐ **D** Just left of the centre line

When you're in a one-way street and want to turn right, you should take up a position in the right-hand lane. This will allow other road users, not wishing to turn, to pass on the left. Indicate your intention and take up the correct position in good time.

57 Mark *one* answer

You wish to turn right ahead. Why should you take up the correct position in good time?

- ☐ **A** To allow other drivers to pull out in front of you
- ☐ **B** To give a better view into the road that you're joining
- ☐ **C** To help other road users know what you intend to do
- ☐ **D** To allow drivers to pass you on the right

If you wish to turn right into a side road, take up your position in good time. Move to the centre of the road when it's safe to do so. This will allow vehicles to pass you on the left. Early planning will show other traffic what you intend to do.

58 Mark *one* answer

At which type of crossing are cyclists allowed to ride across with pedestrians?

- ☐ **A** Toucan
- ☐ **B** Puffin
- ☐ **C** Pelican
- ☐ **D** Zebra

A toucan crossing is designed to allow pedestrians and cyclists to cross at the same time. Look out for cyclists approaching the crossing at speed.

59 Mark *one* answer

You're driving at the legal speed limit. A vehicle comes up quickly behind you, flashing its headlights. What should you do?

- ☐ **A** Accelerate to make a gap behind you
- ☐ **B** Touch the brakes sharply to show your brake lights
- ☐ **C** Maintain your speed to prevent the vehicle from overtaking
- ☐ **D** Allow the vehicle to overtake

Don't enforce the speed limit by blocking another vehicle's progress. This will only lead to the other driver becoming more frustrated. Allow the other vehicle to pass when you can do so safely.

60 Mark *one* answer

When should you flash your headlights at other road users?

- ☐ **A** When showing that you're giving way
- ☐ **B** When showing that you're about to turn
- ☐ **C** When telling them that you have right of way
- ☐ **D** When letting them know that you're there

You should only flash your headlights to warn others of your presence. Don't use them to greet others, show impatience or give priority to other road users, because they could misunderstand your signal.

61 Mark *one* answer

You're approaching an unmarked crossroads. How should you deal with this type of junction?

☐ **A** Accelerate and keep to the middle
☐ **B** Slow down and keep to the right
☐ **C** Accelerate and look to the left
☐ **D** Slow down and look both ways

Be cautious, especially when your view is restricted by hedges, bushes, walls, large vehicles, etc. In the summer months, these junctions can become more difficult to deal with, because growing foliage may further obscure your view.

62 Mark *one* answer

The conditions are good and dry. When should you use the 'two-second rule'?

☐ **A** Before restarting the engine after it has stalled
☐ **B** When checking your gap from the vehicle in front
☐ **C** Before using the 'Mirrors – Signal – Manoeuvre' routine
☐ **D** When traffic lights change to green

In good conditions, the 'two-second rule' can be used to check the distance between your vehicle and the one in front. This technique works on roads carrying faster traffic. Choose a fixed object, such as a bridge, sign or tree. When the vehicle ahead passes this object, say to yourself 'Only a fool breaks the two-second rule.' If you reach the object before you finish saying this, you're too close.

63 Mark *one* answer

At a puffin crossing, which colour follows the green signal?

☐ **A** Steady red
☐ **B** Flashing amber
☐ **C** Steady amber
☐ **D** Flashing green

Puffin crossings have infra-red sensors that detect when pedestrians are crossing and hold the red traffic signal until the crossing is clear. The use of a sensor means there's no flashing amber phase as there is with a pelican crossing.

64 Mark *one* answer

You're in a line of traffic. The driver behind you is following very closely. What action should you take?

☐ **A** Ignore the following driver and continue to travel within the speed limit
☐ **B** Slow down, gradually increasing the gap between you and the vehicle in front
☐ **C** Signal left and wave the following driver past
☐ **D** Move over to a position just left of the centre line of the road

If the driver behind is following too closely, there's a danger they'll collide with the back of your vehicle if you stop suddenly. You can reduce this risk by slowing down and increasing the safety margin in front of you. This reduces the chance that you'll have to stop suddenly and allows you to spread your braking over a greater distance. This is an example of defensive driving.

65 Mark *one* answer

What could happen if you ride your motorcycle when it has a very loose drive chain?

☐ **A** The front wheel could wobble
☐ **B** The ignition could cut out
☐ **C** The brakes could fail
☐ **D** The rear wheel could lock

Drive chains are subject to wear and need frequent adjustment to maintain the correct tension. Allowing the drive chain to run dry will greatly increase the rate of wear, so it's important to keep it lubricated. If the chain becomes worn or slack, it can jump off the sprocket and lock the rear wheel.

66 Mark *one* answer

What's the most important reason why you should keep your motorcycle regularly maintained?

☐ **A** To accelerate faster than other traffic
☐ **B** So the motorcycle can carry panniers
☐ **C** To keep the machine roadworthy
☐ **D** So the motorcycle can carry a passenger

Whenever you use any motorcycle on the road, it must be in a roadworthy condition. Regular maintenance should identify any faults at an early stage and help prevent more serious problems.

67 Mark *one* answer

How should you ride a motorcycle when new tyres have just been fitted?

☐ **A** Carefully, until the shiny surface is worn off
☐ **B** By braking hard, especially into bends
☐ **C** Normally, but with higher tyre pressures
☐ **D** By riding at faster-than-normal speeds

New tyres have a shiny finish, which needs to wear off before the tyre will give the best grip. Take extra care if the road surface is wet or slippery.

68 Mark *one* answer

What will be the effect of wearing brightly coloured clothing while you're riding?

☐ **A** You'll dazzle other road users
☐ **B** You'll be seen more easily by other road users
☐ **C** You'll distract other road users
☐ **D** You'll be able to ride on unlit roads at night with sidelights

For your own safety, you need other road users to see you easily. Wearing brightly coloured or fluorescent clothing will help you to achieve this during daylight. At night, wearing clothing that includes reflective material is the best way of helping others to see you.

69 Mark *one* answer
What should you do when you're riding a motorcycle in very hot weather?

☐ **A** Ride with your visor fully open
☐ **B** Continue to wear protective clothing
☐ **C** Wear trainers instead of boots
☐ **D** Slacken your helmet strap

Always wear your protective clothing, whatever the weather. In very hot weather it's tempting to ride in light summer clothes, but it isn't worth the risk. If you fall from your motorcycle, you'll have no protection from the hard road surface.

70 Mark *one* answer
Why should you wear fluorescent clothing when riding in daylight?

☐ **A** It reduces wind resistance
☐ **B** It prevents injury if you come off the machine
☐ **C** It helps other road users to see you
☐ **D** It keeps you cool in hot weather

Motorcycles are smaller and therefore harder to see than most other vehicles on the road. You need to make yourself as visible as possible to other road users. Fluorescent and reflective clothing will help achieve this. You must be visible from all sides.

71 Mark *one* answer
Why should riders wear reflective clothing?

☐ **A** To protect them from the cold
☐ **B** To protect them from direct sunlight
☐ **C** To be seen better in daylight
☐ **D** To be seen better at night

Fluorescent clothing will help others to see you during the day. At night, however, you should wear clothing that reflects the light. This allows other road users to see you more easily in their headlights. Ask your local motorcycle dealer about fluorescent and reflective clothing.

72 Mark *one* answer
Which fairing would give you the best weather protection?

☐ **A** Handlebar
☐ **B** Sports
☐ **C** Touring
☐ **D** Windscreen

Fairings give protection to the hands, legs and feet. They also make riding more comfortable by keeping you out of the wind.

73 Mark *one* answer

What should you do if your visor becomes badly scratched?

- ☐ **A** Polish it with a fine abrasive
- ☐ **B** Replace it
- ☐ **C** Wash it in soapy water
- ☐ **D** Clean it with petrol

Your visor protects your eyes from wind, rain, insects and road dirt. It's important to keep it clean and in good repair. A badly scratched visor can obscure your view and cause dazzle from the lights of oncoming vehicles.

74 Mark *one* answer

What's the legal minimum depth of tread for motorcycle tyres?

- ☐ **A** 1 mm
- ☐ **B** 1.6 mm
- ☐ **C** 2.5 mm
- ☐ **D** 4 mm

The law says that the entire original tread must be visible, with a depth of at least 1 mm in a continuous band across at least three-quarters of the breadth of the tread. However, your tyres are your only contact with the road, so it's recommended that you replace them before they get to this level.

75 Mark *one* answer

What can you wear to make it easier for other road users to see you?

- ☐ **A** Black leathers
- ☐ **B** Tinted visor
- ☐ **C** White helmet
- ☐ **D** Grey helmet

Many incidents and collisions involving motorcyclists occur because other road users don't see them. Be aware that you're vulnerable and make yourself as visible as possible by wearing fluorescent clothing and a light or brightly coloured helmet.

76 Mark *one* answer

What should you do if the oil-pressure warning light comes on while you're riding?

- ☐ **A** Go to a dealer for an oil change
- ☐ **B** Go to the nearest garage to ask their advice
- ☐ **C** Ride slowly for a few miles to see if the light goes out
- ☐ **D** Stop as soon as possible and try to find the cause

If the oil-pressure warning light comes on when the engine is running, pull over as soon as you can, stop the engine and investigate the cause; if you don't, you risk serious engine damage.

77 Mark *one* answer

What must you check on both the front and rear motorcycle tyres?

☐ **A** That they're the same tread pattern
☐ **B** That they're correctly inflated
☐ **C** That they're the same size
☐ **D** That they're the same make

Your safety and that of others depends on the condition of your tyres. Before every trip, make sure they:
• are correctly inflated
• have at least the minimum legal depth of tread
• have no cuts or bulges.

Do these checks as part of a routine before every journey.

78 Mark *one* answer

What could happen if you ride your motorcycle with a slack or worn drive chain?

☐ **A** The engine could misfire
☐ **B** The tyres could wear more quickly
☐ **C** The engine could produce more emissions
☐ **D** The rear wheel could lock

Check your drive chain regularly; adjust and lubricate it if necessary. It needs to be adjusted until the 'free play' is as it says in the vehicle handbook. If the chain is too loose, it can jump off its sprocket and lock your rear wheel while you're riding.

79 Mark *one* answer

When riding your motorcycle, a tyre bursts. What should you do?

☐ **A** Slow gently to a stop
☐ **B** Brake firmly to a stop
☐ **C** Change to a high gear
☐ **D** Lower the side stand

If a tyre bursts, close the throttle smoothly and slow gently to a stop, holding the handlebars firmly to help you keep a straight course.

80 Mark *one* answer

What will be the effect of having your motorcycle engine properly maintained?

☐ **A** It will use much more fuel
☐ **B** It will have lower exhaust emissions
☐ **C** It will increase your insurance premiums
☐ **D** It will reduce your journey times

A badly maintained engine will emit more exhaust fumes than one that's correctly serviced. This is damaging to the environment. The engine will also use more fuel.

81 Mark *one* answer
What should you clean visors and goggles with?

- ☐ **A** Petrol
- ☐ **B** White spirit
- ☐ **C** Anti-freeze
- ☐ **D** Soapy water

It's very important to keep your visor or goggles clean. Clean them using warm soapy water. Don't use solvents or petrol.

82 Mark *one* answer
You're riding on a quiet road. Your visor fogs up. What should you do?

- ☐ **A** Continue at a reduced speed
- ☐ **B** Stop as soon as possible and wipe it
- ☐ **C** Build up speed to increase the air flow
- ☐ **D** Close the helmet air vents

In cold and wet weather, your visor may fog up. If this happens when you're riding, choose somewhere safe to stop, and wipe it clean with a damp cloth. Special anti-fog products are available at motorcycle dealers.

83 Mark *one* answer
You're riding in hot weather. What's the safest type of footwear?

- ☐ **A** Sandals
- ☐ **B** Trainers
- ☐ **C** Shoes
- ☐ **D** Boots

It's important to wear good boots when you ride a motorcycle. Boots protect your feet and shins from knocks, and give some protection in a crash. They also help keep you warm and dry in cold or wet weather.

84 Mark *one* answer
Which method of fastening your helmet is unsafe?

- ☐ **A** Double D-ring fastening
- ☐ **B** Velcro tab
- ☐ **C** Quick-release fastening
- ☐ **D** Bar and buckle

Some helmet straps have a Velcro tab in addition to the main fastening, which is intended to secure the strap so that it doesn't flap in the wind. It shouldn't be used on its own to fasten the helmet.

85 Mark *one* answer

Your motorcycle has a catalytic converter. What does this reduce?

☐ **A** Exhaust noise
☐ **B** Fuel consumption
☐ **C** Exhaust emissions
☐ **D** Engine noise

Catalytic converters reduce the toxic and polluting gases given out by the engine. Never use leaded or lead-replacement petrol in a motorcycle with a catalytic converter; even one tankful can permanently damage the system.

86 Mark *one* answer

What should you check after refitting your rear wheel?

☐ **A** Your steering damper
☐ **B** Your side stand
☐ **C** Your wheel alignment
☐ **D** Your suspension preload

After refitting the rear wheel or adjusting the drive chain, you should check your wheel alignment. Incorrect alignment will result in excessive tyre wear and poor roadholding.

87 Mark *one* answer

You're checking your direction indicators. How many times per second must they flash?

☐ **A** Between 1 and 2 times
☐ **B** Between 3 and 4 times
☐ **C** Between 5 and 6 times
☐ **D** Between 7 and 8 times

You should check that all your lights work properly before every journey. If you aren't sure whether your signals can be seen, you can use arm signals as well to make your intentions clear; avoid this if you're riding at speed because it can upset your stability.

88 Mark *one* answer

What should you check after adjusting the final drive chain?

☐ **A** The rear wheel alignment
☐ **B** The suspension adjustment
☐ **C** The rear shock absorber
☐ **D** The front suspension forks

Always check the rear wheel alignment after adjusting the final drive chain. Marks on the chain adjuster may be provided to make this easy. Incorrect alignment can cause instability and increased tyre wear.

89 Mark *one* answer
Your steering feels wobbly. Which of these is a likely cause?

- ☐ **A** Tyre pressure is too high
- ☐ **B** Incorrectly adjusted brakes
- ☐ **C** Worn steering-head bearings
- ☐ **D** A broken clutch cable

Worn bearings in the steering head can make your motorcycle very difficult to control. They should be checked for wear or correct adjustment and replaced if necessary.

90 Mark *one* answer
You have a faulty oil seal on a shock absorber. Why is this a serious problem?

- ☐ **A** It will cause excessive chain wear
- ☐ **B** The motorcycle will be difficult to control
- ☐ **C** Your motorcycle will be harder to ride uphill
- ☐ **D** Your motorcycle won't accelerate so quickly

As well as making your motorcycle difficult to control, the leaking oil could find its way onto your tyres and brakes. This could result in a loss of control, putting you and other road users in danger.

91 Mark *one* answer
Oil is leaking from your forks. Why shouldn't you ride a motorcycle in this condition?

- ☐ **A** Your suspension will be ineffective
- ☐ **B** Your steering is likely to seize up
- ☐ **C** The forks will quickly begin to rust
- ☐ **D** The motorcycle will become too noisy

If an oil seal on your forks or shock absorbers fails, fork oil will leak out, making the suspension ineffective and the motorcycle difficult to control. It can also be very dangerous if the oil gets onto brakes or tyres. Replace faulty oil seals without delay.

92 Mark *one* answer
You've adjusted your drive chain. If this isn't done properly, what problem could it cause?

- ☐ **A** Inaccurate speedometer reading
- ☐ **B** Loss of braking power
- ☐ **C** Incorrect rear wheel alignment
- ☐ **D** Excessive fuel consumption

After carrying out drive-chain adjustment, you should always check the rear wheel alignment. Many motorcycles have alignment guides stamped onto the frame to help you do this correctly.

93 Mark *one* answer

There's a cut in the sidewall of one of your tyres. What should you do about this?

- ☐ **A** Replace the tyre before riding the motorcycle
- ☐ **B** Check regularly to see if it gets any worse
- ☐ **C** Repair the cut before riding the motorcycle
- ☐ **D** Reduce the tyre pressure before you ride

A cut in the sidewall can be very dangerous. The tyre is in danger of blowing out if you ride the motorcycle in this condition.

94 Mark *one* answer

You need to put air into your tyres. How would you find out the correct pressure to use?

- ☐ **A** It will be shown on the tyre wall
- ☐ **B** It will be stamped on the wheel
- ☐ **C** By checking the vehicle handbook
- ☐ **D** By checking the registration document

Tyre pressures should be checked regularly. Look in your vehicle handbook for the correct pressures to use.

95 Mark *one* answer

What can you do to prevent a cable-operated clutch from becoming stiff?

- ☐ **A** Keep the cable tight
- ☐ **B** Keep the cable dry
- ☐ **C** Keep the cable slack
- ☐ **D** Keep the cable oiled

Keeping the clutch cable oiled will help it to move smoothly through its outer casing. This will extend the life of the cable and help prevent the clutch's operation from becoming stiff.

96 Mark *one* answer

What can incorrect wheel alignment cause?

- ☐ **A** A serious loss of power
- ☐ **B** Reduced braking performance
- ☐ **C** Increased tyre wear
- ☐ **D** Reduced ground clearance

If a motorcycle's wheels are incorrectly aligned, tyres may wear unevenly and the motorcycle can become unstable, especially when cornering.

97 Mark *one* answer
Why should you wear specialist motorcycle clothing when riding?

□ **A** Because the law requires you to do so
□ **B** Because it looks better than ordinary clothing
□ **C** Because it gives the best protection from the weather
□ **D** Because it will reduce your insurance premium

If you become cold and wet when riding, this can have a serious effect on your concentration and control of your motorcycle. Proper riding gear can help shield you from the weather, as well as giving protection in the event of a crash.

98 Mark *one* answer
What should you do when leaving your motorcycle parked?

□ **A** Remove the battery lead
□ **B** Pull it onto the kerb
□ **C** Use the steering lock
□ **D** Leave the parking lights on

You should always use the steering lock when leaving your motorcycle. Also consider using additional locking devices, such as a U-lock, disc lock or chain. If possible, fasten the motorcycle to an immovable post or another machine.

99 Mark *one* answer
You're parking your motorcycle. How can you reduce the chances of it being stolen?

□ **A** Park in a space marked for motorcycles only
□ **B** Chain it to an immovable object
□ **C** Switch off the engine cut-out switch
□ **D** Leave it on its side stand

Theft of motorcycles is a very common crime. If you can, secure your vehicle to a lamppost or other such object, to help reduce the chances of it being stolen.

100 Mark *one* answer
You're parking your motorcycle and sidecar on a hill. What's the best way to stop it rolling away?

□ **A** Leave it in neutral
□ **B** Put the rear wheel on the pavement
□ **C** Leave it in a low gear
□ **D** Park very close to another vehicle

To make sure a sidecar outfit doesn't roll away after you've parked it, you should leave it in a low gear and wedge it against the kerb or place a block behind the wheel.

101 Mark *one* answer
When would you use the engine cut-out switch?

☐ **A** To reduce speed in an emergency
☐ **B** To prevent the motorcycle being stolen
☐ **C** To stop the engine normally
☐ **D** To stop the engine in an emergency

If you're involved in a collision, using the engine cut-out switch will help to reduce the risk of fire. When stopping the engine normally, use the ignition switch.

102 Mark *one* answer
What should you do when you ride along a road where there are road humps?

☐ **A** Maintain a reduced speed throughout
☐ **B** Accelerate quickly between each one
☐ **C** Always keep to the maximum legal speed
☐ **D** Ride slowly at school times only

The humps are there to reduce the speed of the traffic. Don't accelerate harshly between them, as you'll then have to brake sharply to negotiate the next hump. Harsh braking and acceleration uses more fuel, as well as causing wear and tear to your vehicle.

103 Mark *one* answer
When should you especially check the engine oil level?

☐ **A** Before a long journey
☐ **B** When the engine is hot
☐ **C** Early in the morning
☐ **D** Every 6000 miles

As well as the oil, you'll need to check other items. These include fuel, water and tyres.

104 Mark *one* answer
You service your own motorcycle. How should you get rid of the old engine oil?

☐ **A** Take it to a local-authority site
☐ **B** Pour it down a drain
☐ **C** Tip it into a hole in the ground
☐ **D** Put it into your dustbin

Never pour the oil down any drain. The oil is highly polluting and could harm wildlife. Put it in a container and dispose of it properly at an authorised site.

105 Mark *one* answer
What safeguard could you take against fire risk to your motorcycle?

☐ **A** Keep water levels above maximum
☐ **B** Check out any strong smell of petrol
☐ **C** Avoid riding with a full tank of petrol
☐ **D** Use unleaded petrol

The fuel in your motorcycle can be a dangerous fire hazard. Don't use a naked flame if you can smell fuel, and don't smoke when refuelling.

106 Mark *one* answer
What would make you more visible in daylight?

☐ **A** Wearing a black helmet
☐ **B** Wearing a brightly coloured helmet
☐ **C** Switching off your headlights
☐ **D** Wearing a dark jacket

Wearing bright or fluorescent clothes will help other road users to see you. Wearing a light or brightly coloured helmet can also make you more visible.

107 Mark *one* answer
When is it illegal to ride with a helmet on?

☐ **A** When the helmet isn't fastened correctly
☐ **B** When the helmet is more than four years old
☐ **C** When you've borrowed someone else's helmet
☐ **D** When the helmet doesn't have chin protection

A helmet that's incorrectly fastened or not fastened at all is likely to come off in a crash and will provide little or no protection. By law, you must wear a helmet when riding on the road, and it must be correctly fastened. (Members of the Sikh religion who wear a turban are exempt.)

108 Mark *one* answer
When should you increase the tyre pressures on your motorcycle?

☐ **A** When riding in hot weather
☐ **B** After a long journey
☐ **C** When carrying a heavy load
☐ **D** When riding in wet weather

The vehicle handbook will explain when it's recommended that you increase tyre pressures – for example, when you're carrying extra weight from a passenger or a heavy load.

109 Mark *one* answer
Which of these items must be kept clean?

☐ **A** Number plate
☐ **B** Wheels
☐ **C** Engine
☐ **D** Fairing

Maintenance is a vital part of road safety. Lights, indicators, reflectors and number plates must be kept clean and clear.

110 Mark *one* answer

For what purpose should you use the engine cut-out switch on your motorcycle?

☐ **A** To save wear and tear on the battery
☐ **B** To stop the engine for a short time
☐ **C** To stop the engine in an emergency
☐ **D** To save wear and tear on the ignition

Only use the engine cut-out switch in an emergency. When stopping the engine normally, use the ignition switch. This will remind you to take your keys with you when parking. It could also prevent starting problems if you forget you've left the cut-out switch in the 'off' position.

111 Mark *one* answer

What should you check after you've adjusted the tension on your drive chain?

☐ **A** Rear wheel alignment
☐ **B** Tyre pressures
☐ **C** Valve clearances
☐ **D** Sidelights

Drive chains wear and need frequent adjustment and lubrication. If the drive chain is worn or slack, it can jump off the sprocket and lock the rear wheel. When you've adjusted the chain tension, you need to check the rear wheel alignment. Marks by the chain adjusters may be provided to make this easier.

112 Mark *one* answer

A friend offers you a second-hand safety helmet for you to use. Why may this be a bad idea?

☐ **A** It may be damaged
☐ **B** You'll be breaking the law
☐ **C** You'll affect your insurance cover
☐ **D** It may be a full-face type

A second-hand helmet may look in good condition but it could have received damage that isn't visible externally. A damaged helmet could be unreliable in a crash. Don't take the risk.

113 Mark *one* answer

You're riding a motorcycle with an engine larger than 50 cc. What would make a tyre illegal?

☐ **A** Tread less than 1.6 mm deep
☐ **B** Tread less than 2 mm deep
☐ **C** A large bulge in the sidewall
☐ **D** A stone wedged in the tread

When checking tyres, make sure there are no bulges or cuts in the sidewalls. Keeping your tyres correctly inflated and in good condition is a vital part of maintaining your motorcycle.

114 Mark *one* answer
How should you maintain cable-operated brakes?

☐ **A** By removing all free play at the lever or pedal
☐ **B** By checking them at normal operating temperature
☐ **C** By always fitting new ones for the MOT
☐ **D** By lubricating and adjusting them regularly

Cables will stretch with use and need checking and adjusting regularly. They also need lubricating to prevent friction and wear of the cables and pivots. Don't over-adjust brake cables or the brakes will bind, causing increased fuel consumption, risk of skidding and risk of the brakes overheating.

115 Mark *one* answer
What benefit will you see if you have your motorcycle serviced regularly?

☐ **A** Lower insurance premiums
☐ **B** A refund on your vehicle tax
☐ **C** Increased exhaust emissions
☐ **D** Better fuel economy

Your motorcycle will run much better and its fuel consumption will be lower if you have it serviced regularly. Check at what intervals you should have your motorcycle serviced – this can vary by model or manufacturer. Keep the service record up to date.

116 Mark *one* answer
What could a loose drive chain cause?

☐ **A** A locked rear wheel
☐ **B** Wobbly wheels
☐ **C** A braking fault
☐ **D** Headlight misalignment

A motorcycle chain will stretch as it wears. It may need frequent checking and adjustment to keep the tension correct. In extreme cases, a loose chain can jump off the sprocket and become wedged in the rear wheel. This could cause serious loss of control and result in a crash.

117 Mark *one* answer
Your motorcycle isn't fitted with daytime running lights. When must you use dipped headlights during the day?

☐ **A** On country roads
☐ **B** In poor visibility
☐ **C** On narrow streets
☐ **D** When parking

It's important that other road users can see you clearly at all times. It will help other road users to see you if you use dipped headlights during the day. You must use dipped headlights during the day if visibility is seriously reduced; that is, when you can't see for more than 100 metres (328 feet).

118 Mark *one* answer
When should you consider increasing your tyre pressures?

☐ **A** When riding on a wet road
☐ **B** When carrying a pillion passenger
☐ **C** When travelling on an uneven surface
☐ **D** When riding on twisty roads

Sometimes, manufacturers advise you to increase your tyre pressures for high-speed riding and when carrying extra weight, such as a pillion passenger. This information can be found in the vehicle handbook.

119 Mark *one* answer
You have too much oil in your engine. What could this cause?

☐ **A** Low oil pressure
☐ **B** Engine overheating
☐ **C** Chain wear
☐ **D** Oil leaks

Too much oil in the engine will create excess crankcase pressure. This could damage engine seals and cause oil leaks. Any excess oil should be drained off.

120 Mark *one* answer
You're leaving your motorcycle unattended on a road. When may you leave the engine running?

☐ **A** When parking for less than five minutes
☐ **B** If the battery is flat
☐ **C** When in a 20 mph zone
☐ **D** Not on any occasion

When you leave your motorcycle parked and unattended on a road, switch off the engine, use the steering lock and remove the ignition key. Also take any tank bags, panniers or loose luggage with you, set the alarm if the motorcycle has one, and use an additional lock and chain, or cable lock.

121 Mark *one* answer
You're involved in a crash. What should you do to reduce the risk of fire?

☐ **A** Keep the engine running
☐ **B** Open the choke
☐ **C** Turn the fuel tap to reserve
☐ **D** Use the engine cut-out switch

The engine cut-out switch is used to stop the engine in an emergency. In the event of a crash, this may help to reduce any fire risk.

122 Mark *one* answer
What should you do when riding at night?

☐ **A** Give arm signals
☐ **B** Wear reflective clothing
☐ **C** Wear a tinted visor
☐ **D** Ride in the centre of the road

At night, you should wear clothing with reflective material, to help other road users to see you. If your jacket doesn't have reflective patches, you could wear garments that do, such as

• a hi-visibility vest or tabard
• a reflective belt.

Also use your headlights on dipped or main beam, as appropriate.

123 Mark *one* answer
What's badly affected if the tyres are under-inflated?

☐ **A** Braking
☐ **B** Indicating
☐ **C** Changing gear
☐ **D** Parking

Your tyres are your only contact with the road. To prevent problems with braking and steering, keep your tyres free from defects; they must have sufficient tread depth and be correctly inflated. Correct tyre pressures help reduce the risk of skidding and provide a safer and more comfortable drive or ride.

124 Mark *one* answer
When mustn't you sound your vehicle's horn?

☐ **A** Between 10.00 pm and 6.00 am in a built-up area
☐ **B** At any time in a built-up area
☐ **C** Between 11.30 pm and 7.00 am in a built-up area
☐ **D** Between 11.30 pm and 6.00 am on any road

Every effort must be made to prevent excessive noise, especially in built-up areas at night. Don't rev your engine or sound the horn unnecessarily. It's illegal to sound your horn in a built-up area between 11.30 pm and 7.00 am, except when another road user poses a danger.

125 Mark *one* answer
What makes the vehicle in the picture 'environmentally friendly'?

☐ **A** It's powered by gravity
☐ **B** It's powered by diesel
☐ **C** It's powered by electricity
☐ **D** It's powered by unleaded petrol

Trams are powered by electricity and therefore don't emit exhaust fumes. They ease traffic congestion by offering drivers an alternative to using their car, particularly in busy cities and towns.

126 Mark *one* answer
Why have 'red routes' been introduced in major cities?

☐ **A** To raise the speed limits
☐ **B** To help the traffic flow
☐ **C** To provide better parking
☐ **D** To allow lorries to load more freely

Inconsiderate parking can obstruct the flow of traffic and so make traffic congestion worse. Red routes are designed to prevent this by enforcing strict parking restrictions. Driving slowly in traffic increases fuel consumption and causes a build-up of exhaust fumes.

127 Mark *one* answer
What's the purpose of road humps, chicanes and narrowings?

☐ **A** To separate lanes of traffic
☐ **B** To increase traffic speed
☐ **C** To allow pedestrians to cross
☐ **D** To reduce traffic speed

Traffic-calming measures help to keep vehicle speeds low in congested areas where there are pedestrians and children. A pedestrian is much more likely to survive a collision with a vehicle travelling at 20 mph than they are with a vehicle travelling at 40 mph.

128 Mark *one* answer
It's essential that tyre pressures are checked regularly. When should this be done?

☐ **A** After any lengthy journey
☐ **B** After travelling at high speed
☐ **C** When tyres are hot
☐ **D** When tyres are cold

Check the tyre pressures when the tyres are cold. This will give you a more accurate reading. The heat generated on a long journey will raise the pressure inside the tyre.

129 Mark *one* answer
When will your vehicle use more fuel?

☐ **A** When its tyres are under-inflated
☐ **B** When its tyres are of different makes
☐ **C** When its tyres are over-inflated
☐ **D** When its tyres are new

Check your tyre pressures frequently – normally once a week. If they're lower than those recommended by the manufacturer, there will be more 'rolling resistance'. The engine will have to work harder to overcome this, leading to increased fuel consumption.

130 Mark *one* answer
How should you dispose of a used vehicle battery?

□ **A** Bury it in your garden
□ **B** Put it in the dustbin
□ **C** Take it to a local-authority site
□ **D** Leave it on waste land

Batteries contain acid, which is hazardous, and they must be disposed of safely. This means taking them to an appropriate disposal site.

131 Mark *one* answer
What's most likely to cause high fuel consumption?

□ **A** Poor steering control
□ **B** Accelerating around bends
□ **C** Staying in high gears
□ **D** Harsh braking and accelerating

Accelerating and braking gently and smoothly will help to save fuel and reduce wear on your vehicle. This makes it better for the environment too.

132 Mark *one* answer
The fluid level in your battery is low. What should you top it up with?

□ **A** Battery acid
□ **B** Distilled water
□ **C** Engine oil
□ **D** Engine coolant

Some modern batteries are maintenance-free. Check your vehicle handbook and, if necessary, make sure that the plates in each battery cell are covered with fluid.

133 Mark *one* answer
You're parked on the road at night. Where must you use parking lights?

□ **A** Where there are continuous white lines in the middle of the road
□ **B** Where the speed limit exceeds 30 mph
□ **C** Where you're facing oncoming traffic
□ **D** Where you're near a bus stop

When parking at night, park in the direction of the traffic. This will enable other road users to see the reflectors on the rear of your vehicle. Use your parking lights if the speed limit is over 30 mph.

134 Mark *one* answer
How can you reduce the environmental harm caused by your motor vehicle?

□ **A** Only use it for short journeys
□ **B** Don't service it
□ **C** Drive faster than normal
□ **D** Keep engine revs low

Engines that burn fossil fuels produce exhaust emissions that are harmful to health. The harder you make the engine work, the more emissions it will produce. Engines also use more fuel and produce higher levels of emissions when they're cold. Anything you can do to reduce your use of fossil fuels will help the environment.

135 Mark *one* answer
What can cause excessive or uneven tyre wear?

- ☐ **A** A faulty gearbox
- ☐ **B** A faulty braking system
- ☐ **C** A faulty electrical system
- ☐ **D** A faulty exhaust system

If you see that parts of the tread on your tyres are wearing before others, it may indicate a brake, steering or suspension fault. Regular servicing will help to detect faults at an early stage and this will avoid the risk of minor faults becoming serious or even dangerous.

136 Mark *one* answer
You need to top up your battery. What level should you fill it to?

- ☐ **A** The top of the battery
- ☐ **B** Halfway up the battery
- ☐ **C** Just below the cell plates
- ☐ **D** Just above the cell plates

Top up the battery with distilled water and make sure each cell plate is covered.

137 Mark *one* answer
Before starting a journey, it's wise to plan your route. How can you do this?

- ☐ **A** Look at a map
- ☐ **B** Contact your local garage
- ☐ **C** Look in your vehicle handbook
- ☐ **D** Check your vehicle registration document

Planning your journey before you set out can help to make it much easier and more pleasant, and may help to ease traffic congestion. Look at a map to help you do this. You may need maps of different scales, depending on where and how far you're going. Printing or writing out the route can also help.

138 Mark *one* answer
How can you plan your route before starting a long journey?

- ☐ **A** Check your vehicle handbook
- ☐ **B** Ask your local garage
- ☐ **C** Use a route planner on the internet
- ☐ **D** Consult a travel agent

Various route planners are available on the internet. Most of them give you several options, allowing you to choose between the most direct route and quieter roads. They may also identify rest and fuel stops. Print off the directions and take them with you.

139 Mark *one* answer
Planning your route before setting out can be helpful. How can you do this?

- ☐ **A** Look in a motoring magazine
- ☐ **B** Only visit places you know
- ☐ **C** Try to travel at busy times
- ☐ **D** Print or write down the route

Print or write down your route before setting out. Some places aren't well signed, so including both place names and road numbers in your directions may help you avoid problems en route. Try to get an idea of how far you're going before you leave. You can also recheck the next stage at each rest stop.

140 Mark *one* answer
Why is it a good idea to plan your journey to avoid busy times?

- ☐ **A** You'll have an easier journey
- ☐ **B** You'll have a more stressful journey
- ☐ **C** Your journey time will be longer
- ☐ **D** It will cause more traffic congestion

No-one likes to spend time in traffic queues. Try to avoid busy times related to school or work travel.

141 Mark *one* answer
You avoid busy times when travelling. How will this affect your journey?

- ☐ **A** You're more likely to be held up
- ☐ **B** Your journey time will be longer
- ☐ **C** You'll travel a much shorter distance
- ☐ **D** You're less likely to be delayed

If possible, avoid the early morning, late afternoon and early evening 'rush hour'. Doing this should allow you to travel in a more relaxed frame of mind, concentrate solely on what you're doing and arrive at your destination feeling less stressed.

142 Mark *one* answer
It can be helpful to plan your route before starting a journey. Why should you also plan an alternative route?

- ☐ **A** Your original route may be blocked
- ☐ **B** Your maps may have different scales
- ☐ **C** You may find you have to pay a congestion charge
- ☐ **D** You may get held up by a tractor

It can be frustrating and worrying to find your planned route is blocked by roadworks or diversions. If you've planned an alternative, you'll feel less stressed and more able to concentrate fully on your driving or riding. If your original route is mostly on motorways, it's a good idea to plan an alternative using non-motorway roads. Always carry a map with you just in case you need to refer to it.

143 Mark *one* answer

You're making an appointment and will have to travel a long distance. How should you plan for the journey?

- ☐ **A** Allow plenty of time for the trip
- ☐ **B** Plan to travel at busy times
- ☐ **C** Avoid roads with the national speed limit
- ☐ **D** Prevent other drivers from overtaking

Always allow plenty of time for your journey in case of unforeseen problems. Anything can happen; for example, punctures, breakdowns, road closures, diversions and delays. You'll feel less stressed and less inclined to take risks if you aren't 'pushed for time'.

144 Mark *one* answer

What can rapid acceleration and heavy braking lead to?

- ☐ **A** Reduced pollution
- ☐ **B** Increased fuel consumption
- ☐ **C** Reduced exhaust emissions
- ☐ **D** Increased road safety

Using the controls smoothly can reduce fuel consumption by about 15%, as well as reducing wear and tear on your vehicle. Plan ahead and anticipate changes of speed well in advance. This will reduce the need to accelerate rapidly or brake sharply.

145 Mark *one* answer

Which of these, if allowed to get low, could cause you to crash?

- ☐ **A** Anti-freeze level
- ☐ **B** Brake fluid level
- ☐ **C** Battery water level
- ☐ **D** Radiator coolant level

You should carry out frequent checks on all fluid levels but particularly brake fluid. As the brake pads or shoes wear down, the brake fluid level will drop. If it drops below the minimum mark on the fluid reservoir, air could enter the hydraulic system and lead to a loss of braking efficiency or even complete brake failure.

146 Mark *one* answer
When will your overall stopping distance be longer?

☐ **A** When you're riding at night
☐ **B** When you're riding in fog
☐ **C** When you're riding with a passenger
☐ **D** When you're riding up a hill

When you're carrying a passenger on a motorcycle, the overall weight will be much more than when you're riding alone. This additional weight will make it harder for you to stop quickly in an emergency, so you'll need to increase the distance between your motorcycle and the vehicle in front.

147 Mark *one* answer
What's the safest way to stop on a wet road?

☐ **A** Change gear without braking
☐ **B** Use the back brake only
☐ **C** Use the front brake only
☐ **D** Use both brakes

Motorcyclists need to take extra care when stopping on wet road surfaces. Plan well ahead so that you're able to brake in good time. For maximum stability, you should use both brakes, and brake when your motorcycle is upright and travelling in a straight line.

148 Mark *one* answer
You're riding in heavy rain. Your rear wheel skids as you accelerate. What must you do to regain control?

☐ **A** Change down to a lower gear
☐ **B** Ease off the throttle
☐ **C** Brake to reduce speed
☐ **D** Put your feet down

If you feel your back wheel beginning to skid as you accelerate, ease off the throttle. This will give your rear tyre the chance to grip the road and stop the skid.

149 Mark *one* answer
Before starting a journey in the snow, what should you do?

☐ **A** Consider whether your journey is essential
☐ **B** Try to avoid taking a passenger
☐ **C** Plan a route avoiding towns
☐ **D** Have a hot drink and a meal

Don't ride in snowy or icy conditions unless your journey is essential. If you must go out, try to keep to main roads, which are more likely to be treated and clear.

150 Mark *one* answer
Why should you ride with dipped headlights on in the daytime?

- ☐ **A** They help other road users to see you
- ☐ **B** They mean that you can ride faster
- ☐ **C** Other vehicles will get out of the way
- ☐ **D** So that they're already on when it gets dark

Make yourself as visible as possible, from the side as well as from the front and rear. Having your headlights on, even in good daylight, can help make you more conspicuous.

151 Mark *one* answer
When are motorcyclists allowed to use high-intensity rear fog lights?

- ☐ **A** When a pillion passenger is being carried
- ☐ **B** When they ride a large touring machine
- ☐ **C** When visibility is 100 metres (328 feet) or less
- ☐ **D** When they're riding on the road for the first time

If your motorcycle is fitted with high-intensity rear fog lights, you must only use them when visibility is seriously reduced. That's when you can see no further than 100 metres (328 feet). This rule about high-intensity rear fog lights applies to all motor vehicles.

152 Mark *one* answer
When must you use your headlights?

- ☐ **A** When riding in a group
- ☐ **B** When visibility is poor
- ☐ **C** When carrying a passenger
- ☐ **D** When parked on an unlit road

Your headlights help you to see in the dark, and help other road users to see you. Use your headlights whenever visibility is poor. Using them at other times may also help other road users to see you. On many motorcycles, the headlights are switched on automatically when you start the engine. Most European countries require headlights to be used at all times.

153 Mark *one* answer
You're riding in town at night. The roads are wet after rain. How will the reflections from wet surfaces affect you?

- ☐ **A** They'll make it easier to stop
- ☐ **B** They'll make it harder to accelerate
- ☐ **C** They'll make it easier to see unlit objects
- ☐ **D** They'll make it harder to see unlit objects

After rain, the reflections from wet surfaces will make it hard to see unlit objects. Make sure that your visor or goggles are clean, so your vision is as clear as possible. Pedestrians will be difficult to see, especially if they're wearing dark clothing.

154 Mark *one* answer

You've just ridden through a flood. What should you test when you're clear of the water?

☐ **A** The starter motor
☐ **B** The headlights
☐ **C** The steering
☐ **D** The brakes

Water can make your brakes less effective. If they've been affected, ride slowly while gently applying them until normal braking is restored.

155 Mark *one* answer

How should you ride through flood water?

☐ **A** Quickly, in a high gear
☐ **B** Slowly, in a high gear
☐ **C** Quickly, in a low gear
☐ **D** Slowly, in a low gear

If you have to ride through a flood, ride slowly in a low gear. Keep the engine running fast enough to keep water out of the exhaust. You may need to slip the clutch to do this.

156 Mark *one* answer

How should you ride at night on a busy main road?

☐ **A** With main-beam headlights on at all times
☐ **B** Wearing non-reflective dark clothing
☐ **C** Using dipped-beam headlights
☐ **D** Wearing tinted glasses or a tinted visor

If there's other traffic on the road at night, use your headlights on dipped beam. Only switch to main beam when you won't dazzle other road users. At night, don't wear tinted glasses or contact lenses, or use a tinted visor, because these make it more difficult to see the road ahead.

157 Mark *one* answer

What should you do to help stay safe when you're riding in fog?

☐ **A** Keep close to the vehicle in front
☐ **B** Keep the vehicle in front in view
☐ **C** Keep close to the centre of the road
☐ **D** Keep your visor or goggles clear

You must use your dipped headlights when visibility is seriously reduced. In fog, a film of mist can form over the outside of your visor or goggles. This can further reduce your ability to see. Be aware of this hazard and keep your visor or goggles clear; anti-mist sprays can help.

158 Mark *one* answer

You're riding in heavy rain. Why should you try to avoid this marked area?

- ☐ **A** It's illegal to ride over bus stops
- ☐ **B** The painted lines may be slippery
- ☐ **C** Cyclists may be using the bus stop
- ☐ **D** Only emergency vehicles may drive over bus stops

Painted lines and road markings can be very slippery, especially for motorcyclists. Try to avoid them if you can do so safely.

---

159 Mark *one* answer

What should you do when riding at night?

- ☐ **A** Wear reflective clothing
- ☐ **B** Wear a tinted visor
- ☐ **C** Ride in the middle of the road
- ☐ **D** Always give arm signals

You need to make yourself as visible as possible – from the front and back, and also from the side. Don't just rely on your headlight and tail light. Wear clothing with reflective material, as this stands out in other vehicles' headlights.

160 Mark *one* answer

When riding in extremely cold conditions, what can you do to keep warm?

- ☐ **A** Stay close to the vehicles in front
- ☐ **B** Wear suitable clothing
- ☐ **C** Lie flat on the tank
- ☐ **D** Put one hand on the exhaust pipe

Motorcyclists are exposed to the elements and can become very cold when riding in wintry conditions. It's important to keep warm or your concentration could be affected. The only way to stay warm is to wear suitable clothing. If you do find yourself getting cold, then stop at a suitable place to warm up.

---

161 Mark *one* answer

What can you do to be seen more easily when you're riding at night?

- ☐ **A** Wear reflective clothing
- ☐ **B** Wear waterproof clothing
- ☐ **C** Keep your motorcycle clean
- ☐ **D** Stay well out to the right

It's vital to make yourself as visible as you can. Use the correct lights on your motorcycle. Wear reflective clothing and a light or brightly coloured helmet. Fluorescent clothing is effective in daytime but won't show up as well at night. Most high-visibility clothing will have a combination of fluorescent and reflective materials.

162 Mark *one* answer
When will your overall stopping distance increase?

- ☐ **A** When it's raining
- ☐ **B** When it's sunny
- ☐ **C** When it's dark
- ☐ **D** When it's windy

Extra care should be taken in wet weather. Wet roads will affect the time it takes you to stop: your stopping distance could be as much as doubled.

163 Mark *one* answer
Which road surface is most likely to reduce the stability of your motorcycle?

- ☐ **A** Tarmac
- ☐ **B** Shellgrip
- ☐ **C** Concrete
- ☐ **D** Loose gravel

Some road surfaces can affect the stability of a motorcycle far more than they affect other vehicles. Look out for loose or slippery road surfaces and be aware of any traffic around you. You may need to take avoiding action and change direction quickly.

164 Mark *one* answer
You're riding past queuing traffic. Why should you be more cautious when approaching this road marking?

- ☐ **A** Lorries will be unloading here
- ☐ **B** Schoolchildren will be crossing here
- ☐ **C** Pedestrians will be standing in the road
- ☐ **D** Traffic could be turning here

When riding past queuing traffic, look out for 'keep clear' road markings, which will indicate a side road or entrance on the left. Vehicles may emerge or turn between gaps in the traffic.

165 Mark *one* answer
What can cause your tyres to lose their grip on the road surface and skid?

- ☐ **A** Giving hand signals
- ☐ **B** Riding one-handed
- ☐ **C** Looking over your shoulder
- ☐ **D** Heavy braking

You can cause your motorcycle to skid by heavy braking, as well as excessive acceleration, swerving or changing direction too sharply, and leaning over too far.

166 Mark *one* answer

When riding in heavy rain, a film of water can build up between your tyres and the road. This is known as aquaplaning. What should you do to keep control when aquaplaning occurs?

□ **A** Use your rear brakes gently
□ **B** Steer to the crown of the road
□ **C** Ease off the throttle smoothly
□ **D** Change up to a higher gear

If your motorcycle starts to aquaplane, ease off the throttle smoothly. Don't brake or turn the steering until tyre grip has been restored.

167 Mark *one* answer

After riding through deep water, you notice your scooter brakes aren't working properly. What would be the best way to dry them out?

□ **A** Ride slowly, braking lightly
□ **B** Ride quickly, braking harshly
□ **C** Stop and dry them with a cloth
□ **D** Stop and wait for a few minutes

You can help to dry out brakes by riding slowly and applying light pressure to the brake pedal/lever. Don't ride at normal speeds until they're working normally again.

168 Mark *one* answer

What should you do if you have to ride in foggy weather?

□ **A** Stay close to the centre of the road
□ **B** Switch on only your sidelights
□ **C** Switch on your dipped headlights
□ **D** Ride in the gutter so you can see the kerb

Only travel in fog if your journey is absolutely necessary. Fog is often patchy and visibility can reduce suddenly, without warning, so use your dipped headlights to help others to see you in these difficult conditions.

169 Mark *one* answer

Only a fool breaks the two-second rule.' What does this refer to?

□ **A** The time recommended when using the choke
□ **B** The time gap when following another vehicle in good conditions
□ **C** The time you should allow to restart a stalled engine
□ **D** The time you should keep your foot down at a junction

It's very important that you always leave a safe gap between your motorcycle and any vehicle you're following. In good conditions, you need to leave at least one metre for every mile per hour of your speed, or a two-second time interval.

170 Mark *one* answer
What should a motorcyclist avoid at a mini-roundabout?

☐ **A** Turning right
☐ **B** Using signals
☐ **C** Taking 'lifesavers'
☐ **D** The painted area

Avoid riding over the painted area of a mini-roundabout, as this can become very slippery – especially when wet. At any given moment, only a small part of a motorcycle tyre makes contact with the road, so any reduction in grip can seriously affect stability.

171 Mark *one* answer
You're riding on an exposed stretch of motorway and there's a strong side wind. When should you take extra care?

☐ **A** As you approach a service area
☐ **B** When you overtake a large vehicle
☐ **C** When there's slow queuing traffic
☐ **D** As you approach an exit slip road

Beware of side winds when riding on exposed stretches of road. Take extra care when overtaking large vehicles. As you pass them, you may emerge from their shelter into a gust of wind that can suddenly blow you off course. Bear in mind that strong winds can affect the stability of other road users too.

172 Mark *one* answer
Why should you try to avoid riding over this marked area?

☐ **A** It's illegal to ride over bus stops
☐ **B** It will alter your machine's centre of gravity
☐ **C** Pedestrians may be waiting at the bus stop
☐ **D** A bus may have left patches of oil

Try to anticipate slippery road surfaces. Watch out for oil patches at places where vehicles stop for some time, such as bus stops, lay-bys and busy junctions.

173 Mark *one* answer
Your overall stopping distance comprises thinking distance and braking distance. You're on a good, dry road surface, with good brakes and tyres. What's the typical braking distance at 50 mph?

☐ **A** 14 metres (46 feet)
☐ **B** 24 metres (79 feet)
☐ **C** 38 metres (125 feet)
☐ **D** 55 metres (180 feet)

Various factors – such as weather and road conditions, vehicle condition and loading – affect how long it takes you to stop. You also need to add reaction time to this. The overall stopping distance at 50 mph includes a thinking distance of 15 metres (the reaction time before braking starts) plus your braking distance of 38 metres, giving a typical overall stopping distance of 53 metres (175 feet) in good conditions.

174 Mark *one* answer
By how much can stopping distances increase in icy conditions?

☐ **A** Two times
☐ **B** Three times
☐ **C** Five times
☐ **D** Ten times

Tyre grip is greatly reduced in icy conditions. For this reason, you need to allow up to ten times the stopping distance you would allow on dry roads.

175 Mark *one* answer
In windy conditions, which activity requires extra care?

☐ **A** Using the brakes
☐ **B** Moving off on a hill
☐ **C** Turning into a narrow road
☐ **D** Passing pedal cyclists

Always give cyclists plenty of room when overtaking them. You need to give them even more room when it's windy. A sudden gust could easily blow them off course and into your path.

176 Mark *one* answer
When approaching a right-hand bend, you should keep well to the left. Why is this?

☐ **A** To improve your view of the road
☐ **B** To overcome the effect of the road's slope
☐ **C** To let faster traffic from behind overtake
☐ **D** To be positioned safely if you skid

Doing this will give you an earlier view around the bend and enable you to see any hazards sooner. It also reduces the risk of collision with an oncoming vehicle that may have drifted over the centre line while taking the bend.

177 Mark *one* answer
You've just gone through deep water. What should you do to make sure your brakes are working properly?

☐ **A** Accelerate and keep to a high speed for a short time
☐ **B** Go slowly while gently applying the brakes
☐ **C** Avoid using the brakes at all for a few miles
☐ **D** Stop for at least an hour to allow them time to dry

Water on the brakes will act as a lubricant, causing them to work less efficiently. Using the brakes lightly as you go along will quickly dry them out.

178 Mark *one* answer
In very hot weather the road surface can become soft. What will this affect?

☐ **A** The suspension
☐ **B** The exhaust emissions
☐ **C** The fuel consumption
☐ **D** The tyre grip

If the road surface becomes very hot, it can soften. Tyres are unable to grip a soft surface as well as they can a firm dry one. Take care when cornering and braking.

179 Mark *one* answer
Where are you most likely to be affected by side winds?

☐ **A** On a narrow country lane
☐ **B** On an open stretch of road
☐ **C** On a busy stretch of road
☐ **D** On a long, straight road

In windy conditions, care must be taken on exposed roads. A strong gust of wind can blow you off course. Watch out for other road users who are particularly likely to be affected, such as cyclists, motorcyclists, high-sided lorries and vehicles towing trailers.

180 Mark *one* answer
In good conditions, what's the typical stopping distance at 70 mph?

☐ **A** 53 metres (175 feet)
☐ **B** 60 metres (197 feet)
☐ **C** 73 metres (240 feet)
☐ **D** 96 metres (315 feet)

Note that this is the typical stopping distance. It will take at least this distance to think, brake and stop in good conditions. In poor conditions, it will take much longer.

181 Mark *one* answer
What's the shortest overall stopping distance on a dry road at 60 mph?

☐ **A** 53 metres (175 feet)
☐ **B** 58 metres (190 feet)
☐ **C** 73 metres (240 feet)
☐ **D** 96 metres (315 feet)

This distance is the equivalent of 18 car lengths. Try pacing out 73 metres and then look back. It's probably further than you think.

182 Mark *one* answer

You're following a vehicle at a safe distance on a wet road. Another driver overtakes you and pulls into the gap you've left. What should you do?

- ☐ **A** Flash your headlights as a warning
- ☐ **B** Try to overtake safely as soon as you can
- ☐ **C** Drop back to regain a safe distance
- ☐ **D** Stay close to the other vehicle until it moves on

Wet weather will affect the time it takes for you to stop and can affect your control. Your speed should allow you to stop safely and in good time. If another vehicle pulls into the gap you've left, ease back until you've regained your stopping distance.

183 Mark *one* answer

You're travelling at 50 mph on a good, dry road. What's your typical overall stopping distance?

- ☐ **A** 36 metres (118 feet)
- ☐ **B** 53 metres (175 feet)
- ☐ **C** 75 metres (245 feet)
- ☐ **D** 96 metres (315 feet)

Even in good conditions, it will usually take you further than you think to stop. Don't just learn the figures; make sure you understand how far the distance is.

184 Mark *one* answer

You're on a good, dry road surface. Your brakes and tyres are good. What's the typical overall stopping distance at 40 mph?

- ☐ **A** 23 metres (75 feet)
- ☐ **B** 36 metres (118 feet)
- ☐ **C** 53 metres (175 feet)
- ☐ **D** 96 metres (315 feet)

Stopping distances are affected by a number of variables. These include the type, model and condition of your vehicle, the road and weather conditions, and your reaction time. Look well ahead for hazards and leave enough space between you and the vehicle in front. This should allow you to pull up safely if you have to, without braking sharply.

185 Mark *one* answer

Overall stopping distance is made up of thinking distance and braking distance. You're on a good, dry road surface, with good brakes and tyres. What's the typical braking distance from 50 mph?

- ☐ **A** 14 metres (46 feet)
- ☐ **B** 24 metres (80 feet)
- ☐ **C** 38 metres (125 feet)
- ☐ **D** 55 metres (180 feet)

Be aware that this is just the braking distance. You need to add the thinking distance to this to give the overall stopping distance. At 50 mph, the typical thinking distance will be 15 metres (50 feet), plus a braking distance of 38 metres (125 feet), giving an overall stopping distance of 53 metres (175 feet). The stopping distance could be greater than this, depending on your attention and response to any hazards. These figures are a general guide.

186 Mark *one* answer

In heavy motorway traffic, the vehicle behind you is following too closely. How can you lower the risk of a collision?

- ☐ **A** Increase your distance from the vehicle in front
- ☐ **B** Brake sharply
- ☐ **C** Switch on your hazard warning lights
- ☐ **D** Move onto the hard shoulder and stop

On busy roads, traffic may still travel at high speeds despite being close together. Don't follow the vehicle in front too closely. If a driver behind seems to be 'pushing' you, gradually increase your distance from the vehicle in front by slowing down gently. This will give you more space in front if you have to brake, and will reduce the risk of a collision involving several vehicles.

187 Mark *one* answer

You're following other vehicles in fog. You have your lights on. What else can you do to reduce the chances of being in a collision?

- ☐ **A** Keep close to the vehicle in front
- ☐ **B** Use your main beam instead of dipped headlights
- ☐ **C** Keep up with the faster vehicles
- ☐ **D** Reduce your speed and increase the gap in front

When it's foggy, use dipped headlights. This will help you see and be seen by other road users. If visibility is seriously reduced, consider using front and rear fog lights if you have them. Keep to a sensible speed and don't follow the vehicle in front too closely. If the road is wet and slippery, you'll need to allow twice the normal stopping distance.

188 Mark *one* answer

You're using a contraflow system. What should you do?

- ☐ **A** Choose an appropriate lane in good time
- ☐ **B** Switch lanes at any time to make progress
- ☐ **C** Increase speed to pass through quickly
- ☐ **D** Follow other motorists closely to avoid long queues

In a contraflow system, you'll be travelling close to oncoming traffic and sometimes in narrow lanes. You should get into the correct lane in good time, obey any temporary speed-limit signs and keep a safe separation distance from the vehicle ahead.

189 Mark *one* answer

Where would you expect to see these markers?

- ☐ **A** On a motorway sign
- ☐ **B** On a railway bridge
- ☐ **C** On a large goods vehicle
- ☐ **D** On a diversion sign

These markers must be fitted to vehicles over 13 metres long, large goods vehicles, and rubbish skips placed in the road. They're reflective to make them easier to see in the dark.

190 Mark *one* answer

What's the main hazard shown in this picture?

- ☐ **A** Vehicles turning right
- ☐ **B** Vehicles doing U-turns
- ☐ **C** The cyclist crossing the road
- ☐ **D** Parked cars around the corner

Look at the picture carefully and try to imagine you're there. The cyclist in this picture appears to be trying to cross the road. You must be able to deal with the unexpected, especially when you're approaching a hazardous junction. Look well ahead to give yourself time to deal with any hazards.

191 Mark *one* answer
Which road user has caused a hazard?

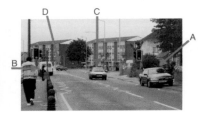

- ☐ **A** The parked car (arrowed A)
- ☐ **B** The pedestrian waiting to cross (arrowed B)
- ☐ **C** The moving car (arrowed C)
- ☐ **D** The car turning (arrowed D)

The car arrowed A is parked within the area marked by zigzag lines at the pedestrian crossing. Parking here is illegal. It also
- blocks the view for pedestrians wishing to cross the road
- restricts the view of the crossing for approaching traffic.

192 Mark *one* answer
What should the driver of the car approaching the crossing do?

- ☐ **A** Continue at the same speed
- ☐ **B** Sound the horn
- ☐ **C** Drive through quickly
- ☐ **D** Slow down and get ready to stop

Look well ahead to see whether any hazards are developing. This will give you more time to deal with them in the correct way. The man in the picture is clearly intending to cross the road. You should be travelling at a speed that allows you to check your mirror, slow down and stop in good time. You shouldn't have to brake harshly.

193 Mark *one* answer

What should the driver of the grey car (arrowed) be especially aware of?

- ☐ **A** The uneven road surface
- ☐ **B** Traffic following behind
- ☐ **C** Doors opening on parked cars
- ☐ **D** Empty parking spaces

When passing parked cars, there's a risk that a driver or passenger may not check before opening the door into the road. A defensive driver will drive slowly and be looking for people who may be about to get out of their car.

194 Mark *one* answer

You see this sign ahead. What should you expect?

- ☐ **A** The road will go steeply uphill
- ☐ **B** The road will go steeply downhill
- ☐ **C** The road will bend sharply to the left
- ☐ **D** The road will bend sharply to the right

This sign indicates that the road will bend sharply to the left. Slow down in plenty of time and select the correct gear before you start to turn. Braking hard and late, while also sharply changing direction, is likely to cause a skid.

195 Mark *one* answer

You're approaching this cyclist. What should you do?

- ☐ **A** Overtake before the cyclist gets to the junction
- ☐ **B** Flash your headlights at the cyclist
- ☐ **C** Slow down and allow the cyclist to turn
- ☐ **D** Overtake the cyclist on the left-hand side

Keep well back and give the cyclist time and room to turn safely. Don't intimidate them by getting too close or trying to squeeze past.

196 Mark *one* answer

Why must you take extra care when turning right at this junction?

- ☐ **A** The road surface is poor
- ☐ **B** The footpaths are narrow
- ☐ **C** The road markings are faint
- ☐ **D** The view is restricted

You may have to pull forward slowly until you can see up and down the road. Be aware that the traffic approaching the junction can't see you either. If you don't know that it's clear, don't go.

197 Mark *one* answer

Which type of vehicle should you be ready to give way to as you approach this bridge?

☐ **A** Bicycles
☐ **B** Buses
☐ **C** Motorcycles
☐ **D** Cars

A double-deck bus or high-sided lorry will have to take a position in the centre of the road to clear the bridge. There's normally a sign to show this. Look well ahead, past the bridge and be ready to stop and give way to large oncoming vehicles.

198 Mark *one* answer

What type of vehicle could you expect to meet in the middle of the road?

☐ **A** Lorry
☐ **B** Bicycle
☐ **C** Car
☐ **D** Motorcycle

The highest point of the bridge is in the centre, so a large vehicle might have to move to the centre of the road to have enough room to pass under the bridge.

199 Mark *one* answer

What must you do at this junction?

☐ **A** Stop behind the line, then edge forward to see clearly
☐ **B** Stop beyond the line, at a point where you can see clearly
☐ **C** Stop only if there's traffic on the main road
☐ **D** Stop only if you're turning right

The 'stop' sign has been put here because the view into the main road is poor. You must stop because it won't be possible to take proper observation while you're moving.

200 Mark *one* answer

A driver pulls out of a side road in front of you, causing you to brake hard. What should you do?

☐ **A** Ignore the error and stay calm
☐ **B** Flash your lights to show your annoyance
☐ **C** Sound your horn to show your annoyance
☐ **D** Overtake as soon as possible

Be tolerant if a vehicle emerges and you have to brake quickly. Anyone can make a mistake, so don't react aggressively. Be alert where there are side roads and be especially careful where there are parked vehicles, because these can make it difficult for emerging drivers to see you.

201 Mark *one* answer
How would age affect an elderly person's driving ability?

- ☐ **A** They won't be able to obtain car insurance
- ☐ **B** They'll need glasses to read road signs
- ☐ **C** They'll take longer to react to hazards
- ☐ **D** They won't signal at junctions

Be tolerant of older drivers. They may take longer to react to a hazard and they may be hesitant in some situations – for example, at a junction.

202 Mark *one* answer
You've just passed these warning lights. What hazard would you expect to see next?

- ☐ **A** A level crossing with no barrier
- ☐ **B** An ambulance station
- ☐ **C** A school crossing patrol
- ☐ **D** An opening bridge

These lights warn that children may be crossing the road to a nearby school. Slow down so that you're ready to stop if necessary.

203 Mark *one* answer
You're planning a long journey. Do you need to plan rest stops?

- ☐ **A** Yes, you should plan to stop every half an hour
- ☐ **B** Yes, regular stops help concentration
- ☐ **C** No, you'll be less tired if you get there as soon as possible
- ☐ **D** No, only fuel stops will be needed

Try to plan your journey so that you can take rest stops. It's recommended that you take a break of at least 15 minutes after every two hours of driving or riding. This should help to maintain your concentration.

204 Mark *one* answer
The red lights are flashing. What should you do when approaching this level crossing?

- ☐ **A** Go through quickly
- ☐ **B** Go through carefully
- ☐ **C** Stop before the barrier
- ☐ **D** Switch on hazard warning lights

At level crossings, the red lights flash before and while the barrier is down. At most crossings, an amber light will precede the red lights. You must stop behind the white line unless you've already crossed it when the amber light comes on. Never zigzag around half-barriers.

205 Mark *one* answer
You're approaching a crossroads. The traffic lights have failed. What should you do?

☐ **A** Brake and stop only for large vehicles
☐ **B** Brake sharply to a stop before looking
☐ **C** Be prepared to brake sharply to a stop
☐ **D** Be prepared to stop for any traffic

When approaching a junction where the traffic lights have failed, you should proceed with caution. Treat the situation as an unmarked junction and be prepared to stop.

206 Mark *one* answer
What should the driver of the red car (arrowed) do?

☐ **A** Wave towards the pedestrians who are waiting to cross
☐ **B** Wait for the pedestrian in the road to cross
☐ **C** Quickly drive behind the pedestrian in the road
☐ **D** Tell the pedestrian in the road she shouldn't have crossed

Some people might take a long time to cross the road. They may be older or have a disability. Be patient and don't hurry them by showing your impatience. If pedestrians are standing at the side of the road, don't signal or wave them to cross. Other road users might not have seen your signal and this could lead the pedestrians into a hazardous situation.

207 Mark *one* answer
You're following a slower-moving vehicle on a narrow country road. There's a junction just ahead on the right. What should you do?

☐ **A** Overtake after checking your mirrors and signalling
☐ **B** Only consider overtaking when you're past the junction
☐ **C** Accelerate quickly to pass before the junction
☐ **D** Slow down and prepare to overtake on the left

You should never overtake as you approach a junction. If a vehicle emerged from the junction while you were overtaking, a dangerous situation could develop very quickly.

208 Mark *one* answer
What should you do as you approach this overhead bridge?

- ☐ **A** Move out to the centre of the road before going through
- ☐ **B** Find another route; this one is only for high vehicles
- ☐ **C** Be prepared to give way to large vehicles in the middle of the road
- ☐ **D** Move across to the right-hand side before going through

Oncoming large vehicles may need to move to the middle of the road to pass safely under the bridge. There won't be enough room for you to continue, so you should be ready to stop and wait.

209 Mark *one* answer
Why are mirrors often slightly curved (convex)?

- ☐ **A** They give a wider field of vision
- ☐ **B** They totally cover blind spots
- ☐ **C** They make it easier to judge the speed of following traffic
- ☐ **D** They make following traffic look bigger

Although a convex mirror gives a wide view of the scene behind, you should be aware that it won't show you everything behind or to the side of your vehicle. Before you move off, you'll need to look over your shoulder to check for anything not visible in the mirrors.

210 Mark *one* answer
A slow-moving lorry showing this sign is travelling in the middle lane of a three-lane motorway. How should you pass it?

- ☐ **A** Cautiously approach the lorry, then pass on either side
- ☐ **B** Don't pass the lorry and leave the motorway at the next exit
- ☐ **C** Use the right-hand lane and pass the lorry normally
- ☐ **D** Approach with care and pass on the left of the lorry

This sign is found on slow-moving or stationary works vehicles. If you wish to overtake, do so on the left, as indicated. Be aware that there might be workmen in the area.

211 Mark *one* answer
You think the driver of the vehicle in front has forgotten to cancel their right indicator. What should you do?

- ☐ **A** Flash your lights to alert the driver
- ☐ **B** Sound your horn before overtaking
- ☐ **C** Overtake on the left if there's room
- ☐ **D** Stay behind and don't overtake

Be cautious and don't attempt to overtake. The driver may be unsure of the location of a junction and may turn suddenly.

212 Mark *one* answer

What's the main hazard the driver of the red car (arrowed) should be aware of?

- ☐ **A** Glare from the sun may affect the driver's vision
- ☐ **B** The black car may stop suddenly
- ☐ **C** The bus may move out into the road
- ☐ **D** Oncoming vehicles will assume the driver is turning right

If you can do so safely, give way to buses signalling to move off at bus stops. Try to anticipate the actions of other road users around you. The driver of the red car should be prepared for the bus pulling out. As you approach a bus stop, look to see how many passengers are waiting to board. If the last one has just got on, the bus is likely to move off.

213 Mark *one* answer

What type of vehicle displays this yellow sign?

- ☐ **A** A broken-down vehicle
- ☐ **B** A school bus
- ☐ **C** An ice-cream van
- ☐ **D** A private ambulance

Buses which carry children to and from school may stop at places other than scheduled bus stops. Be aware that they might pull over at any time to allow children to get on or off. This will normally be when traffic is heavy during rush hour.

214 Mark *one* answer

What hazard should you be aware of when travelling along this street?

- ☐ **A** Glare from the sun
- ☐ **B** Lack of road markings
- ☐ **C** Children running out between vehicles
- ☐ **D** Large goods vehicles

On roads where there are many parked vehicles, you might not be able to see children between parked cars and they may run out into the road without looking.

215 Mark *one* answer
What's the main hazard you should be aware of when following this cyclist?

- ☐ **A** The cyclist may move to the left and dismount
- ☐ **B** The cyclist may swerve into the road
- ☐ **C** The contents of the cyclist's carrier may fall onto the road
- ☐ **D** The cyclist may wish to turn right at the end of the road

When following a cyclist, be aware that they have to deal with the hazards around them. They may wobble or swerve to avoid a pothole in the road or see a potential hazard and change direction suddenly. Don't follow them too closely or rev your engine impatiently.

216 Mark *one* answer
A driver's behaviour has upset you. What can you do to safely get over this incident?

- ☐ **A** Stop and take a break
- ☐ **B** Shout abusive language
- ☐ **C** Gesture to them with your hand
- ☐ **D** Follow them, flashing your headlights

If you feel yourself becoming tense or upset, stop in a safe place and take a break. Tiredness can make things worse and may cause a different reaction to upsetting situations.

217 Mark *one* answer
How should you drive in areas with traffic-calming measures?

- ☐ **A** At a reduced speed
- ☐ **B** At the speed limit
- ☐ **C** In the centre of the road
- ☐ **D** With headlights on dipped beam

Traffic-calming measures such as road humps, chicanes and narrowings are intended to slow drivers down to protect vulnerable road users. Don't speed up until you reach the end of the traffic-calmed zone.

218 Mark *one* answer
When approaching this hazard, why should you slow down?

- ☐ **A** Because of the level crossing
- ☐ **B** Because it's hard to see to the right
- ☐ **C** Because of approaching traffic
- ☐ **D** Because of animals crossing

You should be slowing down and selecting the correct gear in case you have to stop at the level crossing. Look for the signals and be prepared to stop if necessary.

219 Mark *one* answer
Why are place names painted on the road surface?

☐ **A** To restrict the flow of traffic
☐ **B** To warn you of oncoming traffic
☐ **C** To enable you to change lanes early
☐ **D** To prevent you changing lanes

The names of towns and cities may be painted on the road at busy junctions and complex road systems. Their purpose is to let you move into the correct lane in good time, allowing traffic to flow more freely.

220 Mark *one* answer
Some two-way roads are divided into three lanes. Why are these particularly dangerous?

☐ **A** Traffic in both directions can use the middle lane to overtake
☐ **B** Traffic can travel faster in poor weather conditions
☐ **C** Traffic can overtake on the left
☐ **D** Traffic uses the middle lane for emergencies only

If you intend to overtake, you must consider that approaching traffic could be planning the same manoeuvre. When you've considered the situation and decided it's safe, indicate your intentions early. This will show the approaching traffic that you intend to pull out.

221 Mark *one* answer
You're on a dual carriageway. Ahead, you see a vehicle with an amber flashing light. What could this be?

☐ **A** An ambulance
☐ **B** A fire engine
☐ **C** A doctor on call
☐ **D** A disabled person's vehicle

An amber flashing light on a vehicle indicates that it's slow-moving. Battery-powered vehicles used by disabled people are limited to 8 mph. It isn't advisable for them to be used on dual carriageways where the speed limit exceeds 50 mph. If they are, then an amber flashing light must be used.

222 Mark *one* answer
What does this signal from a police officer mean to oncoming traffic?

☐ **A** Go ahead
☐ **B** Stop
☐ **C** Turn left
☐ **D** Turn right

Police officers may need to direct traffic; for example, at a junction where the traffic lights have broken down. Check your copy of *The Highway Code* for the signals that they use.

223 Mark *one* answer
Why should you be cautious when going past this stationary bus?

- ☐ **A** There is traffic approaching in the distance
- ☐ **B** The driver may open the door
- ☐ **C** People may cross the road in front of it
- ☐ **D** The road surface will be slippery

A stationary bus at a bus stop can hide pedestrians who might try to cross the road just in front of it. Drive at a speed that will enable you to respond safely if you have to.

224 Mark *one* answer
Where shouldn't you overtake?

- ☐ **A** On a single carriageway
- ☐ **B** On a one-way street
- ☐ **C** Approaching a junction
- ☐ **D** Travelling up a long hill

You should overtake only when it's really necessary and you can see it's clear ahead. Look out for road signs and markings that show it's illegal or would be unsafe to overtake; for example, approaching junctions or bends. In many cases, overtaking is unlikely to significantly improve your journey time.

225 Mark *one* answer
What's an effect of drinking alcohol?

- ☐ **A** Poor judgement of speed
- ☐ **B** A loss of confidence
- ☐ **C** Faster reactions
- ☐ **D** Greater awareness of danger

Alcohol will severely reduce your ability to drive or ride safely and there are serious consequences if you're caught over the drink-drive limit. It's known that alcohol can
- affect your judgement
- cause overconfidence
- reduce coordination and control.

226 Mark *one* answer
What's likely to happen if you get cold and wet when riding a motorcycle?

- ☐ **A** Your concentration will be impaired
- ☐ **B** Your riding will improve
- ☐ **C** Your visor will freeze up
- ☐ **D** Your reactions will be quicker

When riding, make sure you wear suitable clothing for the conditions. Getting cold and wet will make you uncomfortable. This can cause you to lose concentration and considerably slow down your reaction time. Stop in a safe place to have a hot drink and warm up before this happens.

227 Mark *one* answer

You're about to ride home but you can't find the glasses you need to wear. What should you do?

- ☐ **A** Ride home slowly, keeping to quiet roads
- ☐ **B** Borrow a friend's glasses and use those
- ☐ **C** Ride home at night, so that the lights will help you
- ☐ **D** Find a way of getting home without riding

If you need glasses to bring your eyesight up to the legal standard for driving or riding, you must wear them whenever you ride. Don't be tempted to ride if you've lost or forgotten your glasses; you'll endanger yourself and other road users, and you'll be breaking the law.

---

228 Mark *one* answer

Which of these is an effect of drinking alcohol?

- ☐ **A** Faster reactions
- ☐ **B** Colour blindness
- ☐ **C** Poor judgement
- ☐ **D** Increased concentration

Even a small amount of alcohol will impair a person's judgement. It can increase confidence to a point where a person's behaviour may become 'out of character'. Someone who normally behaves sensibly may take risks and could endanger themselves and others. Don't drink and ride, or accept a lift from anyone who's been drinking.

229 Mark *one* answer

You find that you need glasses to read vehicle number plates at the required distance. When must you wear them?

- ☐ **A** Only in bad weather conditions
- ☐ **B** At all times when riding
- ☐ **C** Only when you think it's necessary
- ☐ **D** Only in bad light or at night time

Have your eyesight tested before you start your practical training. Then have checks periodically throughout your riding life, as your vision may change.

---

230 Mark *one* answer

How are you likely to be affected by drinking alcohol?

- ☐ **A** You'll be more cautious and perceptive
- ☐ **B** The speed of your reactions will increase
- ☐ **C** Your judgement of speed will be worse
- ☐ **D** Your awareness of danger will improve

Never drink if you're going to drive or ride. Your judgement can be seriously affected, even if you aren't over the drink-drive limit. Don't take risks; it isn't worth it.

231 Mark *one* answer
Why should you wear ear plugs when riding a motorcycle?

- ☐ **A** To help prevent hearing damage
- ☐ **B** To make you less aware of traffic
- ☐ **C** To help keep you warm
- ☐ **D** To make your helmet fit better

The use of ear plugs is recommended to protect your hearing from being damaged by the noise of air turbulence around your helmet. Staying within the national speed limit, a rider may experience noise levels in excess of 100 decibels.

232 Mark *one* answer
You're going to a social event and alcohol will be available. You'll be riding your motorcycle shortly afterwards. What's the safest thing to do?

- ☐ **A** Stay just below the legal limit
- ☐ **B** Have soft drinks and alcohol in turn
- ☐ **C** Don't go beyond the legal limit
- ☐ **D** Stick to non-alcoholic drinks

Drinking even the smallest amount of alcohol can affect your judgement and reactions. The safest and best option is to avoid any alcohol at all when riding or driving.

233 Mark *one* answer
You're convicted of riding after drinking too much alcohol. How could this affect your insurance?

- ☐ **A** Your insurance may become invalid
- ☐ **B** The amount of excess you pay will be reduced
- ☐ **C** You'll only be able to get third-party cover
- ☐ **D** Cover will only be given for riding smaller motorcycles

Riding while under the influence of drink or drugs can invalidate your insurance. It also endangers yourself and others. The risk isn't worth taking.

234 Mark *one* answer
You aren't sure whether your cough medicine will affect your ability to ride safely. What should you do?

- ☐ **A** Ask your doctor
- ☐ **B** Don't take the medicine
- ☐ **C** Ride if you feel all right
- ☐ **D** Ask a friend or relative for advice

If you're taking medicine or drugs prescribed by your doctor, check to make sure they won't make you drowsy. If you forget to ask when you're at the surgery, check with your pharmacist.

235 Mark *one* answer
Which arm signal means 'I intend to slow down or stop'?

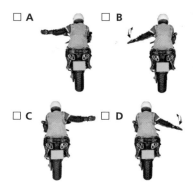

☐ **A**   ☐ **B**

☐ **C**   ☐ **D**

Give your signal in good time and return your hand to the handlebars before changing speed or direction. While you're giving an arm signal you have reduced steering control and you're unable to operate some controls. If you're travelling at speed, it's generally safer to rely on your direction indicators and brake lights.

236 Mark *one* answer
Which type of glasses shouldn't be worn when riding at night?

☐ **A** Half-moon
☐ **B** Round
☐ **C** Bifocal
☐ **D** Tinted

If you're riding at night or in poor visibility, tinted lenses or a tinted visor will reduce the amount of available light reaching your eyes, making you less able to see clearly.

237 Mark *one* answer
In which of these circumstances may you use hazard warning lights?

☐ **A** When riding on a motorway, to warn traffic behind of a hazard ahead
☐ **B** When you're double parked on a two-way road
☐ **C** When your direction indicators aren't working
☐ **D** When riding in town, to warn oncoming traffic that you intend to stop

Hazard warning lights are an important safety feature. Use them when riding on a motorway to warn following traffic of danger ahead. You should also use them if your motorcycle has broken down and is causing an obstruction.

238 Mark *one* answer
Why should you check over your shoulder before turning right into a side road?

☐ **A** To make sure the side road is clear
☐ **B** To check for emerging traffic
☐ **C** To check for overtaking vehicles
☐ **D** To confirm your intention to turn

Take a check over your shoulder before committing yourself to a manoeuvre. This is especially important when turning right, as other road users may not have seen your signal or may not understand your intentions.

239 Mark *one* answer
When should you use hazard warning lights?

☐ **A** When you're double-parked on a two-way road
☐ **B** When your direction indicators aren't working
☐ **C** When warning oncoming traffic that you intend to stop
☐ **D** When your motorcycle has broken down and is causing an obstruction

Hazard warning lights are an important safety feature and should be used if you've broken down and are causing an obstruction. Don't use them as an excuse to park illegally, even for a short time. You may also use them on motorways to warn following traffic of danger ahead.

---

240 Mark *one* answer
It's a very hot day. What would you expect to find?

☐ **A** Mud on the road
☐ **B** A soft road surface
☐ **C** Roadworks ahead
☐ **D** Banks of fog

In very hot weather, the road surface can become soft and may melt. Take care when braking and cornering on soft tarmac, as this can lead to reduced grip and cause skidding.

241 Mark *one* answer

Why should you keep a large gap between your motorcycle and a lorry in front?

- ☐ **A** So you don't breathe in the lorry's exhaust fumes
- ☐ **B** So wind from the lorry won't slow you down
- ☐ **C** So drivers behind can see you
- ☐ **D** So your view ahead isn't obstructed

If you follow a large vehicle too closely, your view beyond it will be restricted. Drop back. This will help you to see more of the road ahead. It will also help the driver of the large vehicle to see you in their mirrors and will give you a safe separation distance if the lorry needs to stop suddenly.

242 Mark *one* answer

You're riding on a country lane. What should you do if you come across cattle on the road?

- ☐ **A** Ride up close behind them
- ☐ **B** Rev your engine
- ☐ **C** Give them plenty of room
- ☐ **D** Sound your horn

Try not to startle the animals. They can be easily frightened by noise or by traffic passing too closely. Slow down, give them plenty of room and be prepared to stop if necessary. Obey any directions given by people in charge of the animals.

243 Mark *one* answer

A learner driver begins to emerge into your path from a side road on the left. What should you do?

- ☐ **A** Be ready to slow down and stop
- ☐ **B** Let them emerge, then ride close behind
- ☐ **C** Turn into the side road
- ☐ **D** Brake hard, then wave them out

You should always be looking for vehicles emerging from side roads as you approach them. If you see another vehicle begin to emerge into your path, be ready to slow down or stop if necessary.

244 Mark *one* answer

The vehicle ahead is being driven by a learner. What should you do?

- ☐ **A** Keep calm and be patient
- ☐ **B** Ride close behind
- ☐ **C** Put your headlights on main beam
- ☐ **D** Sound your horn and overtake

Learner drivers might take longer to react to traffic situations, so be patient and give them time. Don't unnerve them by riding close behind or showing signs of impatience.

245 Mark *one* answer

You're riding in fast-flowing traffic. The vehicle behind is following too closely. What should you do?

- ☐ **A** Slow down gradually to increase the gap in front of you
- ☐ **B** Slow down as quickly as possible by braking
- ☐ **C** Accelerate to get away from the vehicle behind you
- ☐ **D** Apply the brakes sharply to warn the driver behind

By increasing the separation distance between you and the vehicle in front, you have a greater safety margin. If the vehicle in front of you brakes suddenly to avoid a hazard, you'll have time to reduce speed gradually. This will reduce the risk of the close-following vehicle running into you.

246 Mark *one* answer

You're riding towards a zebra crossing. Waiting to cross is a person in a wheelchair. What should you do?

- ☐ **A** Continue on your way
- ☐ **B** Wave to the person to cross
- ☐ **C** Wave to the person to wait
- ☐ **D** Be prepared to stop

As you would with any pedestrian, you should prepare to stop. Don't wave the person across, as other traffic may not slow down.

247 Mark *one* answer

Why should you allow extra room when overtaking another motorcyclist on a windy day?

- ☐ **A** The rider may turn off suddenly to get out of the wind
- ☐ **B** The rider may be blown across in front of you
- ☐ **C** The rider may stop suddenly
- ☐ **D** The rider may be travelling faster than normal

On a windy day, be aware that the blustery conditions might blow you or other motorcyclists out of position. Think about this before deciding to overtake.

248 Mark *one* answer

You've stopped at a pelican crossing, where a disabled person is crossing very slowly in front of you. What should you do when the lights change to green?

- ☐ **A** Allow the person to finish crossing
- ☐ **B** Edge forward slowly
- ☐ **C** Ride behind the person
- ☐ **D** Sound your horn

At a pelican crossing, the green light means you may proceed as long as the crossing is clear. If someone hasn't finished crossing, be patient and wait until the road is clear.

249 Mark *one* answer
Where should you take particular care to look out for other motorcyclists and cyclists?

☐ **A** On dual carriageways
☐ **B** At junctions
☐ **C** At zebra crossings
☐ **D** On one-way streets

Other motorcyclists and cyclists may be difficult to see on the road, particularly at junctions. If your view is blocked by other traffic, you may not be able to see them approaching.

250 Mark *one* answer
Why is it vital for a rider to make a lifesaver check before turning right?

☐ **A** To check for any overtaking traffic
☐ **B** To confirm that they're about to turn
☐ **C** To make sure the side road is clear
☐ **D** To check that the rear indicator is flashing

The lifesaver glance makes you aware of what's happening behind and alongside you before you alter your course. This glance must be timed so that you still have time to react if it isn't safe to carry out your manoeuvre.

251 Mark *one* answer
You're about to overtake a group of horse riders. What's most likely to scare the horses?

☐ **A** Your dipped headlights
☐ **B** Giving arm signals
☐ **C** Riding slowly
☐ **D** Revving your engine

When passing horses, allow them plenty of space and slow down. Animals can be frightened by sudden or loud noises, so don't sound your horn or rev your engine.

252 Mark *one* answer
Young and new motorcyclists are involved in more incidents than other motorcyclists. Why is this?

☐ **A** They use borrowed equipment
☐ **B** They lack experience and judgement
☐ **C** They ride in bad weather conditions
☐ **D** They don't maintain their motorcycles

Young and inexperienced motorcyclists are far more likely to be involved in incidents than more experienced riders. The reasons for this include natural exuberance, showing off, competitive behaviour and overconfidence. Don't overestimate your abilities and never ride too fast for the conditions.

253 Mark *one* answer
What would make a young motorcyclist especially vulnerable?

- ☐ **A** Wearing newer gear than experienced riders
- ☐ **B** Having faster reactions than older riders
- ☐ **C** Overestimating their own ability
- ☐ **D** Getting cheap insurance

Young and inexperienced motorcyclists often have more confidence than ability. It takes time to gain experience and become a good rider. Make sure you have the right attitude and put safety first.

254 Mark *one* answer
The road outside this school is marked with yellow zigzag lines. What do these lines mean?

- ☐ **A** You may park on the lines when dropping off schoolchildren
- ☐ **B** You may park on the lines when picking up schoolchildren
- ☐ **C** You must not wait or park your motorcycle here
- ☐ **D** You must stay with your motorcycle if you park here

Parking here will block the view of the road, endangering the lives of children crossing the road on their way to and from school.

255 Mark *one* answer
Which sign means that there may be people walking along the road?

☐ A   ☐ B

☐ C   ☐ D

Always check the road signs. Triangular signs are warning signs: they inform you about hazards ahead and help you to anticipate any problems. There are a number of different signs showing pedestrians. Learn the meaning of each one.

256 Mark *one* answer
You're turning left at a junction where pedestrians have started to cross. What should you do?

- ☐ **A** Go around them, leaving plenty of room
- ☐ **B** Stop and wave at them to cross
- ☐ **C** Sound your horn and proceed
- ☐ **D** Give way to them

When you're turning into a side road, pedestrians who are crossing have priority. You should wait to allow them to finish crossing safely. Be patient if they're slow or unsteady. Don't try to rush them by sounding your horn, flashing your lights, revving your engine or giving any other inappropriate signal.

257 Mark *one* answer
You're turning left into a side road. What hazard should you be especially aware of?

☐ **A** One-way street
☐ **B** Pedestrians
☐ **C** Traffic congestion
☐ **D** Parked vehicles

Make sure that you've reduced your speed and are in the correct gear for the turn. Look into the road before you turn and always give way to any pedestrians who are crossing.

258 Mark *one* answer
You intend to turn right into a side road. Why should you check for motorcyclists just before turning?

☐ **A** They may be overtaking on your left
☐ **B** They may be following you closely
☐ **C** They may be emerging from the side road
☐ **D** They may be overtaking on your right

Never attempt to change direction to the right without first checking your right-hand mirror and blind spot. A motorcyclist might not have seen your signal and could be hidden by other traffic. This observation should become a matter of routine.

259 Mark *one* answer
Why is a toucan crossing different from other crossings?

☐ **A** Moped riders can use it
☐ **B** It's controlled by a traffic warden
☐ **C** It's controlled by two flashing lights
☐ **D** Cyclists can use it

Toucan crossings are shared by pedestrians and cyclists, who are permitted to cycle across. They're shown the green light together. The signals are push-button-operated and there's no flashing amber phase.

260 Mark *one* answer
How will a school crossing patrol signal you to stop?

☐ **A** By pointing to children on the opposite pavement
☐ **B** By displaying a red light
☐ **C** By displaying a 'stop' sign
☐ **D** By giving you an arm signal

If a school crossing patrol steps out into the road with a 'stop' sign, you must stop. Don't wave anyone across the road and don't get impatient or rev your engine.

261 Mark *one* answer
Where would you see this sign?

- ☐ **A** In the window of a car taking children to school
- ☐ **B** At the side of the road
- ☐ **C** At playground areas
- ☐ **D** On the rear of a school bus or coach

Vehicles that are used to carry children to and from school will be travelling at busy times of the day. If you're following a vehicle with this sign, be prepared for it to make frequent stops. It might pick up or set down passengers in places other than normal bus stops.

262 Mark *one* answer
What does this sign mean?

- ☐ **A** No route for pedestrians and cyclists
- ☐ **B** A route for pedestrians only
- ☐ **C** A route for cyclists only
- ☐ **D** A route for pedestrians and cyclists

This sign shows a shared route for pedestrians and cyclists: when it ends, the cyclists will be rejoining the main road.

263 Mark *one* answer
You see a pedestrian carrying a white stick with a red band. What does this tell you?

- ☐ **A** They have limited mobility
- ☐ **B** They're deaf
- ☐ **C** They're blind
- ☐ **D** They're deaf and blind

When someone is deaf as well as blind, they may carry a white stick with a red reflective band. They may not be aware that you're approaching and they may not be able to hear anything; so, for example, your horn would be ineffective as a warning to them.

264 Mark *one* answer
What action would you take when elderly people are crossing the road?

- ☐ **A** Wave them across so they know that you've seen them
- ☐ **B** Be patient and allow them to cross in their own time
- ☐ **C** Rev the engine to let them know that you're waiting
- ☐ **D** Tap the horn in case they're hard of hearing

Be aware that older people might take a long time to cross the road. They might also be hard of hearing and not hear you approaching. Don't hurry older people across the road by getting too close to them or revving your engine.

265 Mark *one* answer
What should you do when you see two elderly pedestrians about to cross the road ahead?

☐ **A** Expect them to wait for you to pass
☐ **B** Speed up to get past them quickly
☐ **C** Stop and wave them across the road
☐ **D** Be careful; they may misjudge your speed

Older people may have impaired hearing, vision, concentration and judgement. They may also walk slowly and so could take a long time to cross the road.

266 Mark *one* answer
You're coming up to a roundabout. A cyclist is signalling to turn right. What should you do?

☐ **A** Overtake on the right
☐ **B** Give a warning with your horn
☐ **C** Signal the cyclist to move across
☐ **D** Give the cyclist plenty of room

If you're following a cyclist who's signalling to turn right at a roundabout, leave plenty of room. Give them space and time to get into the correct lane.

267 Mark *one* answer
Which of these should you allow extra room when overtaking?

☐ **A** Lorry
☐ **B** Tractor
☐ **C** Bicycle
☐ **D** Road-sweeping vehicle

Don't pass cyclists too closely, as they may
- need to veer around a pothole or other obstacle
- be buffeted by side wind
- be made unsteady by your vehicle.
- Always leave as much room as you would for a car, and don't cut in front of them.

268 Mark *one* answer
Why should you look particularly for motorcyclists and cyclists at junctions?

☐ **A** They may want to turn into the side road
☐ **B** They may slow down to let you turn
☐ **C** They're harder to see
☐ **D** They might not see you turn

Cyclists and motorcyclists are smaller than other vehicles and so are more difficult to see. They can easily be hidden from your view by cars parked near a junction.

269 Mark *one* answer
You're waiting to come out of a side road. Why should you look carefully for motorcycles?

☐ **A** Motorcycles are usually faster than cars
☐ **B** Police patrols often use motorcycles
☐ **C** Motorcycles can easily be hidden behind obstructions
☐ **D** Motorcycles have right of way

If you're waiting to emerge from a side road, look carefully for motorcycles: they can be difficult to see. Be especially careful if there are parked vehicles or other obstructions restricting your view.

270 Mark *one* answer
In daylight, an approaching motorcyclist is using dipped headlights. Why?

☐ **A** So that the rider can be seen more easily
☐ **B** To stop the battery overcharging
☐ **C** To improve the rider's vision
☐ **D** The rider is inviting you to proceed

A motorcycle can be lost from sight behind another vehicle. The use of the headlights helps to make it more conspicuous and therefore more easily seen.

271 Mark *one* answer
Why should motorcyclists wear bright clothing?

☐ **A** They must do so by law
☐ **B** It helps keep them cool in summer
☐ **C** The colours are popular
☐ **D** Drivers often do not see them

Motorcycles and scooters are generally smaller than other vehicles and can be difficult to see. Wearing bright clothing makes it easier for other road users to see a motorcyclist approaching, especially at junctions.

272 Mark *one* answer
You're unsure what a slow-moving motorcyclist ahead of you is going to do. What should you do?

☐ **A** Pass on the left
☐ **B** Pass on the right
☐ **C** Stay behind
☐ **D** Move closer

When a motorcyclist is travelling slowly, it's likely that they're looking for a turning or entrance. Be patient and stay behind them in case they stop or change direction suddenly.

273 Mark *one* answer
Why will a motorcyclist look round over their right shoulder just before turning right?

☐ **A** To listen for following traffic
☐ **B** Motorcycles don't have mirrors
☐ **C** It helps them balance as they turn
☐ **D** To check for traffic in their blind area

When you see a motorcyclist take a glance over their shoulder, they're probably about to change direction. Recognising a clue like this helps you to anticipate their next action. This can improve road safety for you and others.

274 Mark *one* answer
Which is the most vulnerable road user at road junctions?

☐ **A** Car driver
☐ **B** Tractor driver
☐ **C** Lorry driver
☐ **D** Motorcyclist

Pedestrians and riders on two wheels can be harder to see than other road users. Make sure you look for them, especially at junctions. Effective observation, coupled with appropriate action, can save lives.

275 Mark *one* answer
You're approaching a roundabout. There are horses just ahead of you. What should you do?

☐ **A** Sound your horn as a warning
☐ **B** Treat them like any other vehicle
☐ **C** Give them plenty of room
☐ **D** Accelerate past as quickly as possible

Horse riders often keep to the outside of the roundabout even if they're turning right. Give them plenty of room and remember that they may have to cross lanes of traffic.

276 Mark *one* answer
As you approach a pelican crossing, the lights change to green. What should you do if elderly people are halfway across?

☐ **A** Wave them to cross as quickly as they can
☐ **B** Rev your engine to make them hurry
☐ **C** Flash your lights in case they haven't noticed you
☐ **D** Wait patiently because they'll probably take longer to cross

If the lights turn to green, wait for any pedestrians to clear the crossing. Allow them to finish crossing the road in their own time, and don't try to hurry them by revving your engine.

277 Mark *one* answer

There are flashing amber lights under a school warning sign. What action should you take?

- ☐ **A** Reduce speed until you're clear of the area
- ☐ **B** Keep up your speed and sound the horn
- ☐ **C** Increase your speed to clear the area quickly
- ☐ **D** Wait at the lights until they change to green

The flashing amber lights are switched on to warn you that children may be crossing near a school. Slow down and take extra care, as you may have to stop.

278 Mark *one* answer

Why must these road markings be kept clear?

- ☐ **A** To allow schoolchildren to be dropped off
- ☐ **B** To allow teachers to park
- ☐ **C** To allow schoolchildren to be picked up
- ☐ **D** To allow a clear view of the crossing area

The markings are there to show that the area must be kept clear. This is to allow an unrestricted view for
- approaching drivers and riders
- children wanting to cross the road.

279 Mark *one* answer

Where would you see this sign?

- ☐ **A** Near a school crossing
- ☐ **B** At a playground entrance
- ☐ **C** On a school bus
- ☐ **D** At a 'pedestrians only' area

Watch out for children crossing the road from the other side of the bus.

280 Mark *one* answer

You're following two cyclists. They approach a roundabout in the left-hand lane. In which direction should you expect the cyclists to go?

- ☐ **A** Left
- ☐ **B** Right
- ☐ **C** Any direction
- ☐ **D** Straight ahead

Cyclists approaching a roundabout in the left-hand lane may be turning right but may not have been able to get into the correct lane due to heavy traffic. They may also feel safer keeping to the left all the way around the roundabout. Be aware of them and give them plenty of room.

281 Mark *one* answer
You're travelling behind a moped. What should you do when you want to turn left just ahead?

☐ **A** Overtake the moped before the junction
☐ **B** Pull alongside the moped and stay level until just before the junction
☐ **C** Sound your horn as a warning and pull in front of the moped
☐ **D** Stay behind until the moped has passed the junction

Passing the moped and turning into the junction could mean that you cut across the front of the rider. This might force them to slow down, stop or even lose control. Stay behind the moped until it has passed the junction and then you can turn without affecting the rider.

282 Mark *one* answer
You see a horse rider as you approach a roundabout. What should you do if they're signalling right but keeping well to the left?

☐ **A** Proceed as normal
☐ **B** Keep close to them
☐ **C** Cut in front of them
☐ **D** Stay well back

Allow the horse rider to enter and exit the roundabout in their own time. They may feel safer keeping to the left all the way around the roundabout. Don't get up close behind or alongside them, because that would probably upset the horse and create a dangerous situation.

283 Mark *one* answer
How would you react to drivers who appear to be inexperienced?

☐ **A** Sound your horn to warn them of your presence
☐ **B** Be patient and prepare for them to react more slowly
☐ **C** Flash your headlights to indicate that it's safe for them to proceed
☐ **D** Overtake them as soon as possible

Learners might not have confidence when they first start to drive. Allow them plenty of room and don't react adversely to their hesitation. We all learn from experience, but new drivers will have had less practice in dealing with all the situations that might occur.

284 Mark *one* answer
What should you do when you're following a learner driver who stalls at a junction?

☐ **A** Be patient, as you expect them to make mistakes

☐ **B** Stay very close behind and flash your headlights

☐ **C** Start to rev your engine if they take too long to restart

☐ **D** Immediately steer around them and drive on

Learning to drive is a process of practice and experience. Try to understand this and tolerate those who make mistakes while they're learning.

285 Mark *one* answer
You're on a country road. What should you expect to see coming towards you on your side of the road?

☐ **A** Motorcycles
☐ **B** Bicycles
☐ **C** Pedestrians
☐ **D** Horse riders

On a quiet country road, always be aware that there may be a hazard just around the next bend, such as a slow-moving vehicle or pedestrians. Pedestrians are advised to walk on the right-hand side of the road if there's no pavement, so they may be walking towards you on your side of the road.

286 Mark *one* answer
What should you do when following a car driven by an elderly driver?

☐ **A** Expect the driver to drive badly
☐ **B** Flash your lights and overtake
☐ **C** Be aware that their reactions may be slower than yours
☐ **D** Stay very close behind but be careful

You must show consideration to other road users. The reactions of older drivers may be slower and they might need more time to deal with a situation. Be tolerant and don't lose patience or show annoyance.

287 Mark *one* answer
You're following a cyclist. What should you do when you wish to turn left just ahead?

☐ **A** Overtake the cyclist before you reach the junction

☐ **B** Pull alongside the cyclist and stay level until after the junction

☐ **C** Hold back until the cyclist has passed the junction

☐ **D** Go around the cyclist on the junction

Make allowances for cyclists, and give them plenty of room. Don't overtake and then immediately turn left. Be patient and turn behind them when they've passed the junction.

288 Mark *one* answer
A horse rider is in the left-hand lane approaching a roundabout. Where should you expect the rider to go?

☐ **A** In any direction
☐ **B** To the right
☐ **C** To the left
☐ **D** Straight ahead

Horses and their riders move more slowly than other road users. They might not have time to cut across heavy traffic to take up a position in the right-hand lane. For this reason, a horse and rider may approach a roundabout in the left-hand lane even though they're turning right.

289 Mark *one* answer
Powered vehicles used by disabled people are small and hard to see. How do they give early warning when on a dual carriageway?

☐ **A** They'll have a flashing red light
☐ **B** They'll have a flashing green light
☐ **C** They'll have a flashing blue light
☐ **D** They'll have a flashing amber light

Powered vehicles used by disabled people are small, low, hard to see and travel very slowly. On a dual carriageway, a flashing amber light will warn other road users.

290 Mark *one* answer
Where should you never overtake a cyclist?

☐ **A** Just before you turn left
☐ **B** On a left-hand bend
☐ **C** On a one-way street
☐ **D** On a dual carriageway

If you want to turn left and there's a cyclist in front of you, hold back. Wait until the cyclist has passed the junction and then turn left behind them. Don't try to intimidate them by driving too closely.

291 Mark *one* answer
What does a flashing amber beacon mean when it's on a moving vehicle?

☐ **A** The vehicle is slow moving
☐ **B** The vehicle has broken down
☐ **C** The vehicle is a doctor's car
☐ **D** The vehicle belongs to a school crossing patrol

Different coloured beacons warn of different types of vehicle needing special attention. Blue beacons are used on emergency vehicles that need priority. Green beacons are found on doctors' cars. Amber beacons generally denote slower moving vehicles, which are often large. These vehicles are usually involved in road maintenance or local amenities and make frequent stops.

292 Mark *one* answer
What does this sign mean?

- ☐ **A** Contraflow cycle lane
- ☐ **B** With-flow cycle lane
- ☐ **C** Cycles and buses only
- ☐ **D** No cycles or buses

Usually, a picture of a cycle will also be painted on the road, and sometimes the lane will have a different coloured surface. Leave these areas clear for cyclists and don't pass too closely when you overtake.

293 Mark *one* answer
You notice horse riders in front. What should you do first?

- ☐ **A** Pull out to the middle of the road
- ☐ **B** Slow down and be ready to stop
- ☐ **C** Accelerate around them
- ☐ **D** Signal right

Be particularly careful when approaching horse riders – slow down and be prepared to stop. Always pass wide and slowly, and look out for signals given by the riders. Horses are unpredictable: always treat them as potential hazards and take great care when passing them.

294 Mark *one* answer
What's the purpose of these road markings?

- ☐ **A** To ensure children can see and be seen when crossing the road
- ☐ **B** To enable teachers to have clear access to the school
- ☐ **C** To ensure delivery vehicles have easy access to the school
- ☐ **D** To enable parents to pick up or drop off children safely

These markings are found on the road outside schools. Don't stop or park on them, even to set down or pick up children. The markings are there to ensure that drivers, riders, children and other pedestrians have a clear view of the road in all directions.

295 Mark *one* answer
The left-hand pavement is closed due to street repairs. What should you do?

- ☐ **A** Watch out for pedestrians walking in the road
- ☐ **B** Use your right-hand mirror more often
- ☐ **C** Speed up to get past the roadworks more quickly
- ☐ **D** Position close to the left-hand kerb

Where street repairs have closed off pavements, proceed carefully and slowly, as pedestrians might have to walk in the road.

296 Mark *one* answer
What should you do when you're following a motorcyclist along a road that has a poor surface?

☐ **A** Follow closely so they can see you in their mirrors
☐ **B** Overtake immediately to avoid delays
☐ **C** Allow extra room in case they swerve to avoid potholes
☐ **D** Allow the same room as normal to avoid wasting road space

To avoid being unbalanced, a motorcyclist might swerve to avoid potholes and bumps in the road. Be prepared for this and allow them extra space.

---

297 Mark *one* answer
What does this sign tell you?

☐ **A** No cycling
☐ **B** Cycle route ahead
☐ **C** Cycle parking only
☐ **D** End of cycle route

With people's concern today for the environment, cycle routes are being extended in our towns and cities. Respect the presence of cyclists on the road and give them plenty of room if you need to pass.

298 Mark *one* answer
You're approaching this roundabout and see the cyclist signal right. Why is the cyclist keeping to the left?

☐ **A** It's a quicker route for the cyclist
☐ **B** The cyclist is going to turn left instead
☐ **C** The cyclist thinks *The Highway Code* doesn't apply to bicycles
☐ **D** The cyclist is slower and more vulnerable

Cycling in today's heavy traffic can be hazardous. Some cyclists may not feel happy about crossing the path of traffic to take up a position in an outside lane. Be aware of this and understand that, although they're in the left-hand lane, the cyclist might be turning right.

299 Mark *one* answer
What should you do when approaching this crossing?

- ☐ **A** Prepare to slow down and stop
- ☐ **B** Stop and wave the pedestrians across
- ☐ **C** Speed up and pass by quickly
- ☐ **D** Continue unless the pedestrians step out

Be courteous and prepare to stop. Don't wave people across, because this could be dangerous if another vehicle is approaching the crossing.

300 Mark *one* answer
You see a pedestrian with a dog wearing a yellow or burgundy coat. What does this indicate?

- ☐ **A** The pedestrian is elderly
- ☐ **B** The pedestrian is a dog trainer
- ☐ **C** The pedestrian is colour-blind
- ☐ **D** The pedestrian is deaf

Dogs trained to help deaf people have a yellow or burgundy coat. If you see one, you should take extra care, as the pedestrian may not be aware of vehicles approaching.

301 Mark *one* answer
Who may use toucan crossings?

- ☐ **A** Motorcyclists and cyclists
- ☐ **B** Motorcyclists and pedestrians
- ☐ **C** Only cyclists
- ☐ **D** Cyclists and pedestrians

There are some crossings where cycle routes lead cyclists to cross at the same place as pedestrians. These are called toucan crossings. Always look out for cyclists, as they're likely to be approaching faster than pedestrians.

302 Mark *one* answer
Some junctions controlled by traffic lights have a marked area between two stop lines. What's this for?

- ☐ **A** To allow taxis to position in front of other traffic
- ☐ **B** To allow people with disabilities to cross the road
- ☐ **C** To allow cyclists and pedestrians to cross the road together
- ☐ **D** To allow cyclists to position in front of other traffic

These are known as advanced stop lines. When the lights are red (or about to become red), you should stop at the first white line. However, if you've crossed that line as the lights change, you must stop at the second line even if it means you're in the area reserved for cyclists.

303 Mark *one* answer

When you're overtaking a cyclist, you should leave as much room as you would give to a car. What's the main reason for this?

- ☐ **A** The cyclist might speed up
- ☐ **B** The cyclist might get off their bike
- ☐ **C** The cyclist might swerve
- ☐ **D** The cyclist might have to make a left turn

Before overtaking, assess the situation. Look well ahead to see whether the cyclist will need to change direction. Be especially aware of a cyclist approaching parked vehicles, as they'll need to alter course. Don't pass too closely or cut in sharply.

304 Mark *one* answer

What should you do when passing sheep on a road?

- ☐ **A** Briefly sound your horn
- ☐ **B** Go very slowly
- ☐ **C** Pass quickly but quietly
- ☐ **D** Herd them to the side of the road

Slow down and be ready to stop if you see animals in the road ahead. Animals are easily frightened by noise and vehicles passing too close to them. Stop if signalled to do so by the person in charge.

305 Mark *one* answer

At night, you see a pedestrian wearing reflective clothing and carrying a bright red light. What does this mean?

- ☐ **A** You're approaching roadworks
- ☐ **B** You're approaching an organised walk
- ☐ **C** You're approaching a slow-moving vehicle
- ☐ **D** You're approaching a traffic danger spot

The people on the walk should be keeping to the left, but don't assume this. Pass carefully, making sure you have time to do so safely. Be aware that the pedestrians have their backs to you and may not know that you're there.

306 Mark *one* answer

You've just passed your test. How can you reduce your risk of being involved in a collision?

- ☐ **A** By always staying close to the vehicle in front
- ☐ **B** By never going over 40 mph
- ☐ **C** By staying in the left-hand lane on all roads
- ☐ **D** By taking further training

New drivers and riders are often involved in a collision or incident early in their driving career. Due to a lack of experience, they may not react to hazards appropriately. Approved training courses are offered by driver and rider training schools for people who have passed their test but want extra training.

307 Mark *one* answer

You're riding behind a long vehicle. There's a mini-roundabout ahead. The vehicle is signalling left, but it's positioned to the right. What should you do?

- [ ] **A** Sound your horn
- [ ] **B** Overtake on the left
- [ ] **C** Keep well back
- [ ] **D** Flash your headlights

Long vehicles need more room than other vehicles to turn at junctions. The driver may take up a position that seems strange, but they have to do this to ensure their rear wheels don't mount the kerb as they turn. Don't overtake on the left – the driver won't expect you to be there and may not see you. Staying well back will also give you a better view ahead.

308 Mark *one* answer

Why should you be careful when riding on roads where electric trams operate?

- [ ] **A** They can't steer to avoid you
- [ ] **B** They give off harmful exhaust fumes
- [ ] **C** They're noisy and slow
- [ ] **D** They can brake very quickly

Electric trams run on rails and can't deviate from the tracks. Keep a lookout for trams, as they move very quietly and can appear suddenly. Be particularly careful when crossing the rails – they can be very slippery, especially when wet.

309 Mark *one* answer

You're about to overtake a slow-moving motorcyclist. Which one of these signs would make you take special care?

- [ ] **A**
- [ ] **B**
- [ ] **C**
- [ ] **D**

In windy weather, watch out for motorcyclists and also cyclists, as they can be blown sideways into your path. When you pass them, leave plenty of room and check their position in your mirror before pulling back in.

310 Mark *one* answer

You're waiting to emerge left from a minor road. A large vehicle is approaching from the right. You have time to turn, but you should wait. Why?

- [ ] **A** The large vehicle can easily hide an overtaking vehicle
- [ ] **B** The large vehicle can turn suddenly
- [ ] **C** The large vehicle is difficult to steer in a straight line
- [ ] **D** The large vehicle can easily hide vehicles from the left

Large vehicles can hide other vehicles that are overtaking – especially motorcycles, which may be filtering past queuing traffic. You need to be aware of the possibility of hidden vehicles and not assume that it's safe to emerge.

311 Mark *one* answer

You're following a long vehicle. As it approaches a crossroads, it signals left but moves out to the right. What should you do?

☐ **A** Get closer in order to pass it quickly
☐ **B** Stay well back and give it room
☐ **C** Assume the signal is wrong and that it's turning right
☐ **D** Overtake it as it starts to slow down

A long vehicle may need to swing out in the opposite direction as it approaches a turn, to allow the rear wheels to clear the kerb. Don't try to filter through if you see a gap; as the lorry turns, the gap will close.

312 Mark *one* answer

You're following a long vehicle approaching a crossroads. The driver signals right but moves close to the left-hand kerb. What should you do?

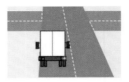

☐ **A** Warn the driver about the wrong signal
☐ **B** Wait behind the long vehicle
☐ **C** Report the driver to the police
☐ **D** Overtake on the right-hand side

When a long vehicle is going to turn right, it may need to keep close to the left-hand kerb. This is to prevent the rear end of the trailer cutting the corner. You need to be aware of how long vehicles behave in such situations. Don't overtake the lorry, because it could turn as you're alongside. Stay behind and wait for it to turn.

313 Mark *one* answer

You're approaching a mini-roundabout. What should you do when you see the long vehicle in front signalling left but positioned over to the right?

- ☐ **A** Sound your horn
- ☐ **B** Overtake on the left
- ☐ **C** Follow the same course as the lorry
- ☐ **D** Keep well back

At mini-roundabouts, there isn't much room for a long vehicle to manoeuvre. It will have to swing out wide so that it can complete the turn safely. Keep well back and don't try to move up alongside it.

314 Mark *one* answer

Before overtaking a large vehicle, you should keep well back. Why is this?

- ☐ **A** To give acceleration space to overtake quickly on blind bends
- ☐ **B** To get the best view of the road ahead
- ☐ **C** To leave a gap in case the vehicle stops and rolls back
- ☐ **D** To offer other drivers a safe gap if they want to overtake you

When following a large vehicle, keep well back. If you're too close, you won't be able to see the road ahead and the driver of the long vehicle might not be able to see you in their mirrors.

315 Mark *one* answer

You're travelling behind a bus that pulls up at a bus stop. What should you do?

- ☐ **A** Accelerate past the bus
- ☐ **B** Watch carefully for pedestrians
- ☐ **C** Sound your horn
- ☐ **D** Pull in closely behind the bus

There might be pedestrians crossing from in front of the bus. Look out for them if you intend to pass. Consider how many people are waiting to get on the bus – check the queue if you can. The bus might move off straight away if no-one is waiting to get on. If a bus is signalling to pull out, give it priority if it's safe to do so.

316 Mark *one* answer

You're following a lorry on a wet road. What should you do when spray makes it difficult to see the road ahead?

- ☐ **A** Drop back until you can see better
- ☐ **B** Put your headlights on full beam
- ☐ **C** Keep close to the lorry, away from the spray
- ☐ **D** Speed up and overtake quickly

Large vehicles throw up a lot of spray when it's wet. This makes it difficult for following drivers to see the road ahead. You'll be able to see more by dropping back further, out of the spray. This will also increase your separation distance, giving you more room to stop if you have to.

317 Mark *one* answer

You keep well back while waiting to overtake a large vehicle. What should you do if a car moves into the gap?

- ☐ **A** Sound your horn
- ☐ **B** Drop back further
- ☐ **C** Flash your headlights
- ☐ **D** Start to overtake

Sometimes your separation distance is shortened by a driver moving into the gap you've allowed. When this happens, react positively, stay calm and drop further back to re-establish a safe following distance.

318 Mark *one* answer

What should you do when you're approaching a bus that's signalling to move away from a bus stop?

- ☐ **A** Get past before it moves
- ☐ **B** Allow it to pull away, if it's safe to do so
- ☐ **C** Flash your headlights as you approach
- ☐ **D** Signal left and wave the bus on

Try to give way to buses if you can do so safely, especially when the driver signals to pull away from a bus stop. Look out for people getting off the bus or running to catch it, because they may cross the road without looking. Don't accelerate to get past the bus, and don't flash your lights, as this could mislead other road users.

319 Mark *one* answer
How should you overtake a long, slow-moving vehicle on a busy road?

☐ **A** Follow it closely and keep moving out to see the road ahead
☐ **B** Flash your headlights for the oncoming traffic to give way
☐ **C** Stay behind until the driver waves you past
☐ **D** Keep well back until you can see that it's clear

When you're following a long vehicle, stay well back so that you can get a better view of the road ahead. The closer you get, the less you'll be able to see of the road. Be patient and don't take a gamble. Only overtake when you're certain that you can complete the manoeuvre safely.

320 Mark *one* answer
Which of these is least likely to be affected by side winds?

☐ **A** Cyclists
☐ **B** Motorcyclists
☐ **C** High-sided vehicles
☐ **D** Cars

Although cars are the least likely to be affected, side winds can take anyone by surprise. This is most likely to happen after overtaking a large vehicle, when passing gaps between hedges or buildings, and on exposed sections of road.

321 Mark *one* answer
What should you do as you approach this lorry?

☐ **A** Slow down and be prepared to wait
☐ **B** Make the lorry wait for you
☐ **C** Flash your lights at the lorry
☐ **D** Move to the right-hand side of the road

When turning, long vehicles need much more room on the road than other vehicles. At junctions, they may take up the whole of the road space, so be patient and allow them the room they need.

322 Mark *one* answer
You're following a large vehicle approaching a crossroads. The driver signals to turn left. What should you do?

☐ **A** Overtake if you can leave plenty of room
☐ **B** Overtake only if there are no oncoming vehicles
☐ **C** Don't overtake until the vehicle begins to turn
☐ **D** Don't overtake as you approach or at the junction

Hold back and wait until the vehicle has turned before proceeding. Don't overtake, because the vehicle turning left could hide a vehicle emerging from the same junction.

323 Mark *one* answer

What's the maximum speed of powered wheelchairs or scooters used by disabled people?

☐ **A** 8 mph
☐ **B** 12 mph
☐ **C** 16 mph
☐ **D** 20 mph

Some powered wheelchairs and mobility scooters are designed for use on the pavement only and cannot exceed 4 mph (6 km/h). Others can go on the road as well, and this category cannot exceed 8 mph (12 km/h). Take great care around these vehicles. They're extremely vulnerable because of their low speed and small size.

324 Mark *one* answer

Why is it more difficult to overtake a large vehicle than a car?

☐ **A** It will take longer to pass one
☐ **B** It will be fitted with a speed limiter
☐ **C** It will have air brakes
☐ **D** It will be slow climbing hills

Depending on relative speed, it will usually take you longer to pass a lorry than other vehicles. Hazards to watch for include oncoming traffic, junctions ahead, bends or dips that could restrict your view, and signs or road markings that prohibit overtaking. Make sure you can see that it's safe to complete the manoeuvre before you start to overtake.

325 Mark *one* answer

When may you overtake another vehicle on the left?

☐ **A** When you're in a one-way street
☐ **B** When approaching a motorway slip road where you'll be turning off
☐ **C** When the vehicle in front is signalling to turn left
☐ **D** When a slower vehicle is travelling in the right-hand lane of a dual carriageway

You may pass slower vehicles on their left while travelling along a one-way street. Be aware of drivers who may need to change lanes and may not expect faster traffic passing on their left.

326 Mark *one* answer

You're travelling in very heavy rain. How is this likely to affect your overall stopping distance?

☐ **A** It will be doubled
☐ **B** It will be halved
☐ **C** It will be ten times greater
☐ **D** It will be no different

The road will be very wet and spray from other vehicles will reduce your visibility. Tyre grip will also be reduced, increasing your stopping distance. You should at least double your separation distance.

327 Mark *one* answer

What should you do when you're overtaking at night?

☐ **A** Wait until a bend so that you can see oncoming headlights
☐ **B** Sound your horn twice before moving out
☐ **C** Put your headlights on full beam
☐ **D** Beware of bends in the road ahead

Don't overtake if there's a possibility of a road junction, bend or brow of a bridge or hill ahead. There are many hazards that are difficult to see in the dark. Only overtake if you're certain that the road ahead is clear. Don't take a chance.

328 Mark *one* answer

When may you wait in a box junction?

☐ **A** When you're stationary in a queue of traffic
☐ **B** When approaching a pelican crossing
☐ **C** When approaching a zebra crossing
☐ **D** When oncoming traffic prevents you turning right

The purpose of a box junction is to keep the junction clear by preventing vehicles from stopping in the path of crossing traffic. You mustn't enter a box junction unless your exit is clear. However, you may enter the box and wait if you want to turn right and are only prevented from doing so by oncoming traffic.

329 Mark *one* answer

Which of these plates normally appears with this road sign?

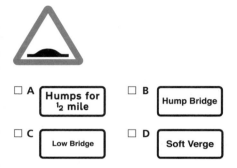

☐ **A** Humps for ½ mile

☐ **B** Hump Bridge

☐ **C** Low Bridge

☐ **D** Soft Verge

Road humps are used to slow down traffic. They're found in places where there are often pedestrians, such as

• shopping areas
• near schools
• residential areas.

Watch out for people close to the kerb or crossing the road.

330 Mark *one* answer

What do traffic-calming measures do?

☐ **A** Stop road rage
☐ **B** Make overtaking easier
☐ **C** Slow traffic down
☐ **D** Make parking easier

Traffic-calming measures make the roads safer for vulnerable road users, such as cyclists, pedestrians and children. These can be designed as chicanes, road humps or other obstacles that encourage drivers and riders to slow down.

331 Mark *one* answer

You're on a motorway in fog. The left-hand edge of the motorway can be identified by reflective studs. What colour are they?

☐ **A** Green
☐ **B** Amber
☐ **C** Red
☐ **D** White

Be especially careful if you're on a motorway in fog. Reflective studs are there to help you in poor visibility. Different colours are used so that you'll know which lane you're in. These are

• red on the left-hand edge of the carriageway
• white between lanes
• amber on the right-hand edge of the carriageway
• green between the carriageway and slip roads.

332 Mark *one* answer
What's a rumble device designed to do?

☐ **A** Give directions
☐ **B** Prevent cattle escaping
☐ **C** Alert you to low tyre pressure
☐ **D** Alert you to a hazard

A rumble device consists of raised markings or strips across the road, designed to give drivers an audible, visual and tactile warning. These devices are used in various locations, including in the line separating the hard shoulder and the left-hand lane on the motorway and on the approach to some hazards, to alert drivers to the need to slow down.

333 Mark *one* answer
What should you do when making a journey in foggy conditions?

☐ **A** Follow other vehicles' tail lights closely
☐ **B** Avoid using dipped headlights
☐ **C** Leave plenty of time for your journey
☐ **D** Keep two seconds behind the vehicle ahead

If you're planning to make a journey when it's foggy, listen to the weather reports. If visibility is very poor, avoid making unnecessary journeys. If you do travel, leave plenty of time – and if someone is waiting for you to arrive, let them know that your journey will take longer than normal. This will also take off any pressure you may feel to rush.

334 Mark *one* answer
What must you do when overtaking a car at night?

☐ **A** Flash your headlights before overtaking
☐ **B** Select a higher gear
☐ **C** Switch your lights to full beam before overtaking
☐ **D** Make sure you don't dazzle other road users

To prevent your lights from dazzling the driver of the car in front, wait until you've passed them before switching to full beam.

335 Mark *one* answer
You're travelling on a road that has speed humps. What should you do when the driver in front is travelling more slowly than you?

☐ **A** Sound your horn
☐ **B** Overtake as soon as you can
☐ **C** Flash your headlights
☐ **D** Slow down and stay behind

Be patient and stay behind the car in front. You shouldn't normally overtake other vehicles in areas subject to traffic calming. If you overtake here, you may easily exceed the speed limit, defeating the purpose of the traffic-calming measures.

336 Mark *one* answer
You see these markings on the road. Why are they there?

- ☐ **A** To show a safe distance between vehicles
- ☐ **B** To keep the area clear of traffic
- ☐ **C** To make you aware of your speed
- ☐ **D** To warn you to change direction

These lines may be painted on the road on the approach to a roundabout, a village or a particular hazard. The lines are raised and painted yellow, and their purpose is to make you aware of your speed. Reduce your speed in good time so that you avoid having to brake harshly over the last few metres before reaching the junction.

337 Mark *one* answer
How would you identify a section of road used by trams?

- ☐ **A** There would be metal studs around it
- ☐ **B** There would be zigzag markings alongside it
- ☐ **C** There would be a different surface texture
- ☐ **D** There would be yellow hatch markings around it

Trams may run on roads used by other vehicles and pedestrians. The section of road used by trams is known as the reserved area and should be kept clear. It usually has a different surface, edged with white lane markings.

338 Mark *one* answer
What should you do when you meet an oncoming vehicle on a single-track road?

- ☐ **A** Reverse back to the main road
- ☐ **B** Carry out an emergency stop
- ☐ **C** Stop at a passing place
- ☐ **D** Switch on your hazard warning lights

Take care when using single-track roads. It can be difficult to see around bends, because of hedges or fences, so expect to meet oncoming vehicles. Drive carefully and be ready to pull into or stop opposite a passing place, where you can pass each other safely.

339 Mark *one* answer
The road is wet. Why might a motorcyclist steer round drain covers on a bend?

- ☐ **A** To avoid puncturing the tyres on the edge of the drain covers
- ☐ **B** To prevent the motorcycle sliding on the metal drain covers
- ☐ **C** To help judge the bend using the drain covers as marker points
- ☐ **D** To avoid splashing pedestrians on the pavement

Other drivers or riders may have to change course due to the size or characteristics of their vehicle. Understanding this will help you to anticipate their actions. Motorcyclists and cyclists will be checking the road ahead for uneven or slippery surfaces, especially in wet weather. They may need to move across their lane to avoid surface hazards such as potholes and drain covers.

340 Mark *one* answer

After this hazard you should test your brakes. Why is this?

- ☐ **A** You'll be on a slippery road
- ☐ **B** Your brakes will be soaking wet
- ☐ **C** You'll be going down a long hill
- ☐ **D** You'll have just crossed a long bridge

A ford is a crossing over a stream that's shallow enough to drive or ride through. After you've gone through a ford or deep puddle, your brakes will be wet and they won't work as well as usual. To dry them out, apply a light brake pressure while moving slowly. Don't travel at normal speeds until you're sure your brakes are working properly again.

341 Mark *one* answer

Why should you always reduce your speed when travelling in fog?

- ☐ **A** The brakes don't work as well
- ☐ **B** You'll be dazzled by other headlights
- ☐ **C** The engine will take longer to warm up
- ☐ **D** It's more difficult to see what's ahead

You won't be able to see as far ahead in fog as you can on a clear day. You'll need to reduce your speed so that, if a hazard looms out of the fog, you have the time and space to take avoiding action. Travelling in fog is hazardous. If you can, try to delay your journey until it has cleared.

342 Mark *one* answer

What safety measure should you take before starting a motorcycle engine?

- ☐ **A** Check that the neutral lamp shows when the ignition is switched on
- ☐ **B** Select first gear and apply the rear brake lightly
- ☐ **C** Select first gear and apply the front brake firmly
- ☐ **D** Check that your dipped headlights and tail light are on

Before starting the engine, make sure the motorcycle is in neutral. Do this by checking that the neutral warning light is lit when you switch on the ignition. If no neutral light is fitted, push the motorcycle forward to check that the rear wheel turns freely.

343 Mark *one* answer
You're the motorcyclist approaching this junction. What should you do?

- ☐ **A** Stop, as the car has right of way
- ☐ **B** Slow down and be ready to stop
- ☐ **C** Dip your headlights and keep near the left-hand kerb
- ☐ **D** Speed up to clear the junction without delay

Look out for road signs warning of side roads, even if you aren't turning off. A driver who's emerging may not be able to see you due to parked cars or heavy traffic. Slow down and be prepared to stop if necessary. Remember, no-one has priority at an unmarked crossroads.

344 Mark *one* answer
What can motorcyclists do to improve their safety on the road?

- ☐ **A** Anticipate the actions of others
- ☐ **B** Stay just above the speed limit
- ☐ **C** Keep positioned close to the kerb
- ☐ **D** Remain well below the speed limit

Always ride defensively. This means looking and planning ahead, as well as anticipating the actions of other road users.

345 Mark *one* answer
What can cause skidding?

- ☐ **A** Braking too gently
- ☐ **B** Feathering the throttle
- ☐ **C** Staying upright when cornering
- ☐ **D** Braking too hard

To keep control of your motorcycle and prevent skidding, you should plan well ahead and avoid late, harsh braking. Try to avoid braking while changing direction, as the tyres may not have enough grip to cope with both together. Always consider how the road and weather conditions may affect your tyres' grip.

346 Mark *one* answer

It's very cold and the road looks wet. What should you do if you can't hear any road noise as you ride?

- ☐ **A** Continue riding at the same speed
- ☐ **B** Ride slowly in as high a gear as possible
- ☐ **C** Ride in as low a gear as possible
- ☐ **D** Brake sharply to see if the road is slippery

Frozen rain on the road is called black ice. It can be hard to see, but it can be indicated by a lack of road noise and your steering may also feel very light. Reduce your speed and avoid harsh braking or steering. Riding in as high a gear as possible can help reduce the risk of wheelspin.

347 Mark *one* answer

When should you wear full protective clothing while riding a motorcycle?

- ☐ **A** At all times
- ☐ **B** Only on faster, open roads
- ☐ **C** Just on long journeys
- ☐ **D** Only during bad weather

Protective clothing is designed to protect you from the cold and wet. It also gives you some protection from injury, so it's important that you always wear protective clothing when you ride.

348 Mark *one* answer

What should you do before you start a journey in foggy conditions?

- ☐ **A** Make sure that you have a spare visor with you
- ☐ **B** Make sure that you have a warm drink with you
- ☐ **C** Check that your lights are working
- ☐ **D** Check that the battery is fully charged

It's best to avoid riding in foggy weather. However, if you have to, there are some precautions you can take before setting off to help make your journey as safe as possible. These include checking that all your lights are clean and working, and that your visor is clean.

349 Mark *one* answer

Where's the best place to park your motorcycle?

- ☐ **A** On soft tarmac
- ☐ **B** On bumpy ground
- ☐ **C** On grass
- ☐ **D** On firm, level ground

Parking your motorcycle on soft ground might cause the stand to sink in, and the machine could fall over. The ground should be level, as well as firm, to keep the motorcycle stable. Use off-road parking or motorcycle parking areas when they're available.

350 Mark *one* answer
What should you do when riding in windy conditions?

☐ **A** Stay close to large vehicles
☐ **B** Keep your speed up
☐ **C** Keep your speed down
☐ **D** Stay close to the gutter

Strong winds can blow a motorcycle off course, and even across the road. In windy conditions, you need to slow down and avoid riding on exposed roads. You should also watch for gaps in buildings and hedges, where you may be affected by a sudden gust of wind.

351 Mark *one* answer
On the road, what should be your normal riding position?

☐ **A** Close to the kerb
☐ **B** In the centre of your lane
☐ **C** On the right of your lane
☐ **D** Near the centre of the road

When you're riding a motorcycle, it's very important to ride where other road users can see you. In normal weather, you should ride in the centre of your lane. This will help you avoid uneven road surfaces in the gutter, and allow others to overtake on the right if they wish.

352 Mark *one* answer
Your motorcycle is parked on a two-way road. How should you get on the machine?

☐ **A** From the right and apply the rear brake
☐ **B** From the left and leave the brakes alone
☐ **C** From the left and apply the front brake
☐ **D** From the right and leave the brakes alone

When you get onto a motorcycle, you should get on from the left side to avoid putting yourself in danger from passing traffic. You should also apply the front brake to prevent the motorcycle from rolling either forwards or backwards.

353 Mark *one* answer
How should you gain basic skills in motorcycle riding?

☐ **A** Practise off-road with an approved training body
☐ **B** Ride on the road on the first dry day
☐ **C** Practise off-road in a public park or in a quiet cul-de-sac
☐ **D** Ride on the road as soon as possible

All new motorcyclists must complete a course of basic training with an approved training body before going on the road. This training is given on a site that's been authorised by the Driver and Vehicle Standards Agency as being suitable for off-road training.

354 Mark *one* answer

What will happen if you ride with your clutch lever pulled in for longer than is necessary?

- ☐ **A** It will increase wear on the gearbox
- ☐ **B** It will increase petrol consumption
- ☐ **C** It will reduce your control of the motorcycle
- ☐ **D** It will reduce the grip of the tyres

Riding with the clutch lever pulled in is known as coasting. If you coast, you lose the benefits of engine braking and you'll have reduced control of your motorcycle.

355 Mark *one* answer

What's most likely to cause a motorcycle to skid?

- ☐ **A** Riding in wet weather
- ☐ **B** Catching your foot on the ground
- ☐ **C** Cornering too fast
- ☐ **D** Riding in the winter

Skids are a lot easier to get into than they are to get out of. Riding at a suitable speed for the conditions, planning, looking ahead for hazards and braking in good time will all help you to avoid skidding or losing control.

356 Mark *one* answer

Your motorcycle doesn't have linked brakes. In an emergency, what should you do to stop quickly?

- ☐ **A** Apply the rear brake only
- ☐ **B** Apply the front brake only
- ☐ **C** Apply the front brake just before the rear brake
- ☐ **D** Apply the rear brake just before the front brake

You should plan ahead to avoid the need to stop suddenly, but if an emergency arises, you must be able to stop safely. Applying the front brake just before the rear brake will help you to stop safely and quickly.

357 Mark *one* answer

What will happen if you look down at the front wheel while riding?

- ☐ **A** It will make your steering lighter
- ☐ **B** It will improve your balance
- ☐ **C** You'll use less fuel
- ☐ **D** You'll upset your balance

When riding, look ahead and around you. Don't look down at the front wheel, as this can severely upset your balance.

358 Mark *one* answer

In normal riding conditions, how should you brake?

- ☐ **A** By using the rear brake first and then the front
- ☐ **B** When the motorcycle is being turned or ridden through a bend
- ☐ **C** By pulling in the clutch before using the front brake
- ☐ **D** When the motorcycle is upright and moving in a straight line

A motorcycle is most stable when it's upright and moving in a straight line. This is the best time to brake. With independent front and rear brakes, both brakes should be used, with the front brake being applied just before the rear brake.

359 Mark *one* answer

Which of these will affect the stopping distance of your motorcycle?

- ☐ **A** The drive-chain adjustment
- ☐ **B** The condition of the tyres
- ☐ **C** The time of day
- ☐ **D** The street lighting

Tyres are a major factor in the handling, stability and stopping distance of a motorcycle. Make sure they're in a safe and legal condition. The weather and road surface also play a part. Always anticipate well ahead and take account of the conditions when you're braking.

360 Mark *one* answer

You're on a motorway at night. In which situation may you have your headlights switched off?

- ☐ **A** When there are vehicles close in front of you
- ☐ **B** When you're travelling below 50 mph
- ☐ **C** When the motorway is lit
- ☐ **D** When your motorcycle is broken down on the hard shoulder

Always use your headlights at night on a motorway, unless you've had to stop on the hard shoulder. If you have to use the hard shoulder, switch off your headlights but leave your parking lights on, so that your motorcycle can be seen by other road users.

361 Mark *one* answer

You have to park on the road in fog. What should you do?

- ☐ **A** Leave parking lights on
- ☐ **B** Leave no lights on
- ☐ **C** Leave dipped headlights on
- ☐ **D** Leave main-beam headlights on

If you have to park on the road in foggy conditions, it's important that your motorcycle can be seen by other road users. Try to find a place to park off the road. If this isn't possible, leave your motorcycle facing in the same direction as the traffic. Make sure that your lights are clean and leave your parking lights on.

362 Mark *one* answer

You're riding on a wet road. What technique should you use when braking?

- ☐ **A** Apply the rear brake well before the front brake
- ☐ **B** Apply the front brake just before the rear brake
- ☐ **C** Avoid using the front brake at all
- ☐ **D** Avoid using the rear brake at all

On wet roads, you'll need to brake earlier and more smoothly than on dry roads. Always try to brake when the motorcycle is upright. This is particularly important in wet conditions.

363 Mark *one* answer

You have to brake sharply and your motorcycle starts to skid. What should you do?

- ☐ **A** Continue braking and select a low gear
- ☐ **B** Apply the brakes harder for better grip
- ☐ **C** Select neutral and use the front brake only
- ☐ **D** Release and reapply the brakes

If you skid as a result of braking harshly, you need to ease off the brakes to stop the skid. You should then reapply them progressively to stop.

364 Mark *one* answer

Traction control systems (TCS) are fitted to some motorcycles. What do they help to prevent?

- ☐ **A** Wheelspin when accelerating
- ☐ **B** Skidding when braking too hard
- ☐ **C** Uneven front tyre wear
- ☐ **D** Uneven rear tyre wear

TCS helps to prevent the rear wheel from spinning, especially when accelerating on a slippery surface.

365 Mark *one* answer

Braking too hard has caused both wheels to skid. What should you do?

- ☐ **A** Release both brakes together
- ☐ **B** Release the front brake, then the rear brake
- ☐ **C** Release the front brake only
- ☐ **D** Release the rear brake only

Braking too hard will cause a skid. Release the brakes immediately to allow the wheels to turn, then reapply them as firmly as the road surface and conditions will allow.

366 Mark *one* answer
Your motorcycle doesn't have linked brakes. What should you do when braking normally to a stop?

☐ **A** Apply only the front brake
☐ **B** Apply only the rear brake
☐ **C** Apply both brakes smoothly
☐ **D** Apply either of the brakes gently

In normal riding, you should always use both brakes. Braking when the motorcycle is upright and travelling in a straight line helps you to keep control. If your motorcycle has linked brakes, refer to the vehicle handbook.

367 Mark *one* answer
You're sitting on a stationary motorcycle and checking your riding position. What should you be able to do?

☐ **A** Just touch the ground with your toes
☐ **B** Place both feet on the ground
☐ **C** Operate the centre stand
☐ **D** Adjust your mirrors by stretching

When sitting astride a stationary motorcycle, you should be able to place both feet on the ground. This should enable you to keep your balance while using one foot to operate the foot controls.

368 Mark *one* answer
It's been raining after a long dry spell. How will this affect the road surface?

☐ **A** It will be rough
☐ **B** It will be flooded
☐ **C** It will be sticky
☐ **D** It will be slippery

During a long spell of hot, dry weather, the road surface will become coated with rubber and dust. When it rains after this, the road surface will be unusually slippery. Take extra care, particularly at junctions, bends and roundabouts, and allow double the usual stopping distance.

369 Mark *one* answer
Riding with the side stand down could cause you to crash. When is this most likely to happen?

☐ **A** When you're going uphill
☐ **B** When you're accelerating
☐ **C** When you're braking
☐ **D** When you're cornering

Cornering with the side stand down could lead to a serious crash. Many motorcycles have a device that stops the engine if you try to ride off with the side stand down, but don't rely on this.

370 Mark *one* answer

You're approaching a road with a surface of loose chippings. What should you do?

☐ **A** Ride normally
☐ **B** Speed up
☐ **C** Slow down
☐ **D** Stop suddenly

The handling of your motorcycle will be greatly affected by the road surface. Look well ahead and be especially alert if the road looks uneven or has loose chippings. Slow down in good time, as braking harshly in these conditions will cause you to skid. For the same reason, avoid making sudden changes of direction.

371 Mark *one* answer

It rains after a long, dry, hot spell. How can this affect the road surface?

☐ **A** It can become unusually slippery
☐ **B** It can give better grip
☐ **C** It can become covered in grit
☐ **D** It can melt and break up

Oil and rubber can build up on the road during long spells of dry weather. When it rains, this can make the road surface very slippery.

372 Mark *one* answer

You ride over broken glass and get a puncture. What should you do?

☐ **A** Close the throttle and roll to a stop
☐ **B** Brake to a stop as quickly as possible
☐ **C** Release your grip on the handlebars
☐ **D** Steer from side to side to keep your balance

Your motorcycle will be very unstable if a tyre bursts. Try to keep a straight course and stop as gently as possible.

373 Mark *one* answer

Spilt fuel on the road can be very dangerous for a motorcyclist. How can this hazard be seen?

☐ **A** By a rainbow-coloured pattern on the road surface
☐ **B** By a series of skid marks on the road surface
☐ **C** By a pitted road surface
☐ **D** By a highly polished road surface

This rainbow-coloured pattern can be seen much more easily on a wet road. You should avoid riding over spilt fuel if possible. If you have to go over it, do so with extreme caution, knowing the surface will be slippery.

374 Mark *one* answer
Which type of road surface increases the risk of skidding for motorcyclists?

☐ **A** Tar banding
☐ **B** Dry tarmac
☐ **C** Concrete
☐ **D** Asphalt

When riding, it's important to look for
• potholes
• drain covers (especially when they're wet)
• tar banding
• oily and greasy surfaces
• road markings
• tram tracks
• wet mud and leaves.

Keen observation will give you more time to brake or change course if you need to avoid these slippery surfaces.

375 Mark *one* answer
The road is wet. You're passing a line of queuing traffic and riding on the painted road markings. What should you take particular care in doing?

☐ **A** Signalling
☐ **B** Braking
☐ **C** Carrying a passenger
☐ **D** Checking your mirrors

When they're wet, painted road markings can be more slippery than the normal road surface. Other road-surface hazards that become slippery when wet include drain covers, leaves and mud. Take extra care when braking or cornering on these wet surfaces.

376 Mark *one* answer
Why should you be careful when crossing tram lines?

☐ **A** Tram lines are always 'live'
☐ **B** Trams will be stopping here
☐ **C** Pedestrians will be crossing here
☐ **D** The steel rails can be slippery

The smooth steel surface can be slippery and dangerous for motorcyclists, especially when it's wet. Try to cross tram lines at right angles.

377 Mark *one* answer
You see a rainbow-coloured pattern on the road. What will this warn you of?

☐ **A** A soft, uneven road surface
☐ **B** A polished road surface
☐ **C** Fuel spilt on the road
☐ **D** Water on the road

If fuel, especially diesel, is spilt on the road, it will make the surface very slippery. In wet weather, it can be seen as a rainbow-coloured pattern on the road.

378 Mark *one* answer

When may you stop on the hard shoulder of a motorway?

- ☐ **A** Only in an emergency
- ☐ **B** If you feel tired and need to rest
- ☐ **C** If you've gone past your exit
- ☐ **D** To answer your mobile phone

You mustn't stop on the hard shoulder, except in an emergency. Never use the hard shoulder to have a rest or a picnic, answer a mobile phone or check a road map. Also, you mustn't travel back along the hard shoulder if you've gone past your exit.

379 Mark *one* answer

You're riding on the motorway. Well before you reach your intended exit, where should you position your motorcycle?

- ☐ **A** In the middle lane
- ☐ **B** In the left-hand lane
- ☐ **C** On the hard shoulder
- ☐ **D** In any lane

You'll see the first advance direction sign one mile from a motorway exit. If you're travelling at 60 mph, you'll only have about 50 seconds before you reach the countdown markers. There'll be another sign at the half-mile point. Move to the left-hand lane in good time. Don't cut across traffic at the last moment and don't risk missing your exit.

380 Mark *one* answer

You're joining a motorway from a slip road. What should you do?

- ☐ **A** Adjust your speed to the speed of the traffic on the motorway
- ☐ **B** Accelerate as quickly as you can and ride straight out
- ☐ **C** Ride onto the hard shoulder until a gap appears
- ☐ **D** Expect drivers on the motorway to give way to you

Give way to vehicles that are already on the motorway, and join the left-hand lane when there's a suitable gap in the traffic. Don't expect traffic on the motorway to give way to you, but try to avoid stopping at the end of the slip road.

381 Mark *one* answer

If you want to ride on the motorway, what's the minimum engine size your motorcycle must have?

- ☐ **A** 50 cc
- ☐ **B** 125 cc
- ☐ **C** 150 cc
- ☐ **D** 250 cc

Riders of motorcycles with an engine smaller than 50 cc aren't allowed to use motorways, due to their restricted speed. They may cause a hazard – both for the rider and for drivers of other vehicles.

382 Mark *one* answer

You're riding at 70 mph on a three-lane motorway. There's no traffic ahead. Which lane should you use?

☐ **A** Any lane
☐ **B** The middle lane
☐ **C** The right-hand lane
☐ **D** The left-hand lane

Use the left-hand lane if it's free, regardless of the speed at which you're travelling.

383 Mark *one* answer   **NI**

You're riding on a motorway. Unless signs show otherwise, what's the national speed limit?

☐ **A** 50 mph
☐ **B** 60 mph
☐ **C** 70 mph
☐ **D** 80 mph

The national speed limit of 70 mph applies to cars and motorcycles on the motorway, unless they're towing a trailer. On smart motorways, this speed limit can be reduced and overhead signs will show the new limit in force.

384 Mark *one* answer

Why is it particularly important to carry out a check of your motorcycle before making a long motorway journey?

☐ **A** You'll have to do more harsh braking on motorways
☐ **B** Motorway service stations don't deal with breakdowns
☐ **C** The road surface will wear down the tyres faster
☐ **D** Continuous high speeds increase the risk of your motorcycle breaking down

Before starting a motorway journey, make sure your motorcycle can cope with the demands of high-speed riding. Things you need to check include oil, water, tyres and fuel. When you're travelling a long way, it's a good idea to plan rest stops in advance.

385 Mark *one* answer

What should you do when you're joining a motorway?

☐ **A** Use the hard shoulder
☐ **B** Stop at the end of the acceleration lane
☐ **C** Slow to a stop before joining the motorway
☐ **D** Give way to traffic already on the motorway

You should give way to traffic already on the motorway. Where possible, traffic may move over to let you in, but don't force your way into the traffic stream. Traffic could be travelling at high speed, so try to match your speed to filter in without affecting the traffic flow.

386 Mark *one* answer
What's the national speed limit on motorways for cars and motorcycles?

- ☐ **A** 30 mph
- ☐ **B** 50 mph
- ☐ **C** 60 mph
- ☐ **D** 70 mph

Travelling at the national speed limit doesn't allow you to hog the right-hand lane. Always use the left-hand lane whenever possible. When leaving a motorway, get into the left-hand lane well before your exit. Reduce your speed on the slip road and look out for sharp bends or curves and traffic queuing at roundabouts.

387 Mark *one* answer
Which vehicles should use the left-hand lane on a three-lane motorway?

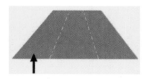

- ☐ **A** Any vehicle
- ☐ **B** Large vehicles only
- ☐ **C** Emergency vehicles only
- ☐ **D** Slow vehicles only

On a motorway, all traffic should use the left-hand lane unless overtaking. When overtaking a number of slower vehicles, move back to the left-hand lane when you're safely past. Check your mirrors frequently and don't stay in the middle or right-hand lane if the left-hand lane is free.

388 Mark *one* answer
Which of these isn't allowed to travel in the right-hand lane of a three-lane motorway?

- ☐ **A** A small delivery van
- ☐ **B** A motorcycle
- ☐ **C** A vehicle towing a trailer
- ☐ **D** A motorcycle and sidecar

A vehicle with a trailer is restricted to 60 mph. For this reason, it isn't allowed in the right-hand lane, as it might hold up faster-moving traffic that wishes to overtake in that lane.

389 Mark *one* answer
You break down on a motorway. You need to call for help. Why may it be better to use an emergency roadside telephone rather than a mobile phone?

- ☐ **A** It connects you to a local garage
- ☐ **B** Using a mobile phone will distract other drivers
- ☐ **C** It allows easy location by the emergency services
- ☐ **D** Mobile phones don't work on motorways

On a motorway, it's best to use a roadside emergency telephone so that the emergency services are able to find you easily. The location of the nearest telephone is shown by an arrow on marker posts at the edge of the hard shoulder. If you use a mobile, the operator will need to know your exact location. Before you call, find out the number on the nearest marker post. This number will identify your exact location.

390   Mark *one* answer

You've had a breakdown on the hard shoulder of a motorway. When the problem has been fixed, how should you rejoin the main carriageway?

☐ **A** Move out onto the carriageway, then build up your speed

☐ **B** Move out onto the carriageway using your hazard warning lights

☐ **C** Gain speed on the hard shoulder before moving out onto the carriageway

☐ **D** Wait on the hard shoulder until someone flashes their headlights at you

Signal your intention and build up sufficient speed on the hard shoulder so that you can filter into a safe gap in the traffic. Don't push your way in, causing other traffic to alter speed or direction.

391   Mark *one* answer

You're travelling along a motorway. Where would you find a crawler or climbing lane?

☐ **A** On a steep gradient
☐ **B** Before a service area
☐ **C** Before a junction
☐ **D** Along the hard shoulder

Large, slow-moving vehicles can hinder the progress of other traffic. On a steep gradient, an extra crawler lane may be provided for slow-moving vehicles to allow faster-moving traffic to flow more easily.

392   Mark *one* answer

What do these motorway signs show?

☐ **A** They're countdown markers to a bridge
☐ **B** They're distance markers to the next telephone
☐ **C** They're countdown markers to the next exit
☐ **D** They warn of a police control ahead

The exit from a motorway is indicated by countdown markers. These are positioned 90 metres (100 yards) apart, the first being 270 metres (300 yards) from the start of the slip road. Move into the left-hand lane well before you reach the start of the slip road.

393   Mark *one* answer

On which part of a motorway are amber reflective studs found?

☐ **A** Between the hard shoulder and the carriageway

☐ **B** Between the acceleration lane and the carriageway

☐ **C** Between the central reservation and the carriageway

☐ **D** Between each pair of lanes

On motorways, reflective studs of various colours are fixed in the road between the lanes. These help you to identify which lane you're in when it's dark or in poor visibility. Amber-coloured studs are found on the right-hand edge of the main carriageway, next to the central reservation.

394 Mark *one* answer

What colour are the reflective studs between the lanes on a motorway?

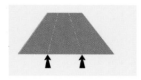

- ☐ **A** Green
- ☐ **B** Amber
- ☐ **C** White
- ☐ **D** Red

White studs are found between the lanes on motorways. They reflect back the light from your headlights. This is especially useful in bad weather, when visibility is restricted.

395 Mark *one* answer

What colour are the reflective studs between a motorway and its slip road?

- ☐ **A** Amber
- ☐ **B** White
- ☐ **C** Green
- ☐ **D** Red

The studs between the carriageway and the hard shoulder are normally red. These change to green where there's a slip road, helping you to identify slip roads when visibility is poor or when it's dark.

396 Mark *one* answer

You've broken down on a motorway. In which direction should you walk to find the nearest emergency telephone?

- ☐ **A** With the traffic flow
- ☐ **B** Facing oncoming traffic
- ☐ **C** In the direction shown on the marker posts
- ☐ **D** In the direction of the nearest exit

Along the hard shoulder there are marker posts at 100-metre intervals. These will direct you to the nearest emergency telephone.

397 Mark *one* answer

You're joining a motorway. Why is it important to make full use of the slip road?

- ☐ **A** Because there is space available to turn round if you need to
- ☐ **B** To allow you direct access to the overtaking lanes
- ☐ **C** To build up a speed similar to traffic on the motorway
- ☐ **D** Because you can continue on the hard shoulder

Try to join the motorway without affecting the progress of the traffic already travelling on it. Always give way to traffic already on the motorway. At busy times you may have to slow down to merge into slow-moving traffic.

398 Mark *one* answer
How should you use the emergency telephone on a motorway?

☐ **A** Stay close to the carriageway
☐ **B** Face the oncoming traffic
☐ **C** Keep your back to the traffic
☐ **D** Stand on the hard shoulder

Traffic is passing you at speed. If the draught from a large lorry catches you by surprise, it could blow you off balance and even onto the carriageway. By facing the oncoming traffic, you can see approaching lorries and so be prepared for their draught. You'll also be in a position to see other hazards approaching.

399 Mark *one* answer
You're on a motorway. What colour are the reflective studs on the left of the carriageway?

☐ **A** Green
☐ **B** Red
☐ **C** White
☐ **D** Amber

Red studs are placed between the edge of the carriageway and the hard shoulder. Where slip roads leave or join the motorway, the studs are green.

400 Mark *one* answer
On a three-lane motorway, which lane should you normally use?

☐ **A** Left
☐ **B** Right
☐ **C** Centre
☐ **D** Either the right or centre

On a three-lane motorway, you should travel in the left-hand lane unless you're overtaking. This applies regardless of the speed at which you're travelling.

401 Mark *one* answer
What should you do when going through a contraflow system on a motorway?

☐ **A** Ensure that you don't exceed 30 mph
☐ **B** Keep a good distance from the vehicle ahead
☐ **C** Switch lanes to keep the traffic flowing
☐ **D** Stay close to the vehicle ahead to reduce queues

At roadworks, and especially where a contraflow system is operating, a speed restriction is likely to be in place. Keep to the lower speed limit and don't
  • switch lanes
  • get too close to the vehicle in front of you
Be aware that there will be no permanent barrier between you and the oncoming traffic.

402 Mark *one* answer

You're on a three-lane motorway. There are red reflective studs on your left and white ones to your right. Which lane are you in?

- ☐ **A** In the right-hand lane
- ☐ **B** In the middle lane
- ☐ **C** On the hard shoulder
- ☐ **D** In the left-hand lane

The colours of the reflective studs on the motorway and their locations are
- red – between the hard shoulder and the carriageway
- white – between lanes
- amber – between the carriageway and the central reservation
- green – along slip-road exits and entrances
- bright green/yellow – at roadworks and contraflow systems.

403 Mark *one* answer

You're approaching roadworks on a motorway. What should you do?

- ☐ **A** Speed up to clear the area quickly
- ☐ **B** Always use the hard shoulder
- ☐ **C** Obey all speed limits
- ☐ **D** Stay very close to the vehicle in front

Collisions often happen at roadworks. Be aware of the speed limits, slow down in good time and keep your distance from the vehicle in front.

404 Mark *one* answer

Which vehicles are prohibited from using the motorway?

- ☐ **A** Powered mobility scooters
- ☐ **B** Motorcycles over 50 cc
- ☐ **C** Double-deck buses
- ☐ **D** Cars with automatic transmission

Motorways mustn't be used by pedestrians, cyclists, motorcycles under 50 cc, certain slow-moving vehicles without permission, and powered wheelchairs/mobility scooters.

405 Mark *one* answer

What should you do when driving or riding along a motorway?

- ☐ **A** Look much further ahead than you would on other roads
- ☐ **B** Travel much faster than you would on other roads
- ☐ **C** Maintain a shorter separation distance than you would on other roads
- ☐ **D** Concentrate more than you would on other roads

Traffic on motorways usually travels faster than on other roads. You need to be looking further ahead to give yourself more time to react to any hazard that may develop.

406 Mark *one* answer
What should you do immediately after joining a motorway?

- ☐ **A** Try to overtake
- ☐ **B** Re-adjust your mirrors
- ☐ **C** Position your vehicle in the centre lane
- ☐ **D** Keep in the left-hand lane

Stay in the left-hand lane long enough to get used to the higher speeds of motorway traffic before considering overtaking.

407 Mark *one* answer
What's the right-hand lane used for on a three-lane motorway?

- ☐ **A** Emergency vehicles only
- ☐ **B** Overtaking
- ☐ **C** Vehicles towing trailers
- ☐ **D** Coaches only

You should keep to the left and only use the right-hand lane if you're passing slower-moving traffic.

408 Mark *one* answer
What should you use the hard shoulder of a motorway for?

- ☐ **A** Stopping in an emergency
- ☐ **B** Leaving the motorway
- ☐ **C** Stopping when you're tired
- ☐ **D** Joining the motorway

Don't use the hard shoulder for stopping unless it's an emergency. If you want to stop for any other reason, go to the next exit or service station.

409 Mark *one* answer
You're in the right-hand lane of a three-lane motorway. What do these overhead signs mean?

- ☐ **A** Move to the left and reduce your speed to 50 mph
- ☐ **B** There are roadworks 50 metres (55 yards) ahead
- ☐ **C** Use the hard shoulder until you've passed the hazard
- ☐ **D** Leave the motorway at the next exit

You must obey these signs even if there appear to be no problems ahead. There could be queuing traffic or another hazard which you can't yet see.

410 Mark *one* answer

When are you allowed to stop on a motorway?

- ☐ **A** When you need to walk and get fresh air
- ☐ **B** When you wish to pick up hitchhikers
- ☐ **C** When you're signalled to do so by flashing red lights
- ☐ **D** When you need to use a mobile telephone

You must stop if overhead gantry signs show flashing red lights above every lane on the motorway. If any of the other lanes doesn't show flashing red lights or a red cross, you may move into that lane and continue if it's safe to do so.

411 Mark *one* answer

You're travelling in the left-hand lane of a three-lane motorway. How should you react to traffic joining from a slip road?

- ☐ **A** Race the other vehicles
- ☐ **B** Move to another lane
- ☐ **C** Maintain a steady speed
- ☐ **D** Switch on your hazard warning lights

Plan well ahead when approaching a slip road. If you see traffic joining the motorway, move to another lane if it's safe to do so. This can help the flow of traffic joining the motorway, especially at peak times.

412 Mark *one* answer

What basic rule applies when you're using a motorway?

- ☐ **A** Use the lane that has the least traffic
- ☐ **B** Keep to the left-hand lane unless overtaking
- ☐ **C** Overtake on the side that's clearest
- ☐ **D** Try to keep above 50 mph to prevent congestion

You should normally travel in the left-hand lane unless you're overtaking a slower-moving vehicle. When you've finished overtaking, move back into the left-hand lane, but don't cut across in front of the vehicle that you've overtaken.

413 Mark *one* answer

You're travelling along a motorway. When are you allowed to overtake on the left?

- ☐ **A** When you can see well ahead that the hard shoulder is clear
- ☐ **B** When the traffic in the right-hand lane is signalling right
- ☐ **C** When you warn drivers behind by signalling left
- ☐ **D** When in queues and traffic to your right is moving more slowly than you are

Never overtake on the left, unless the traffic is moving in queues and the queue on your right is moving more slowly than the one you're in.

414 Mark *one* answer

On a motorway, what's an emergency refuge area used for?

☐ **A** In cases of emergency or breakdown
☐ **B** If you think you'll be involved in a road rage incident
☐ **C** For a police patrol to park and watch traffic
☐ **D** For construction and road workers to store emergency equipment

Emergency refuge areas are built at the side of the hard shoulder. If you break down, try to get your vehicle into the refuge, where there's an emergency telephone. The phone connects directly to a control centre. Remember to take care when rejoining the motorway, especially if the hard shoulder is being used as a running lane.

415 Mark *one* answer

Traffic officers operate on motorways and some primary routes in England. What are they authorised to do?

☐ **A** Stop and arrest drivers who break the law
☐ **B** Repair broken-down vehicles on the motorway
☐ **C** Issue fixed penalty notices
☐ **D** Stop and direct anyone on a motorway

Traffic officers don't have enforcement powers but are able to stop and direct people on motorways and some 'A' class roads. They only operate in England and work in partnership with the police at incidents, providing a highly trained and visible service. They're recognised by an orange-and-yellow jacket and their vehicle has yellow-and-black markings.

416 Mark *one* answer

You're on a motorway. A red cross is displayed above the hard shoulder. What does this mean?

☐ **A** Pull up in this lane to answer your mobile phone
☐ **B** Use this lane as a running lane
☐ **C** This lane can be used if you need a rest
☐ **D** You shouldn't travel in this lane

Active traffic management operates on some motorways. Within these areas, at certain times, the hard shoulder will be used as a running lane. A red cross above the hard shoulder shows that this lane should only be used for emergencies and breakdowns.

417 Mark *one* answer
You're on a smart motorway. A mandatory speed limit is displayed above the hard shoulder. What does this mean?

- ☐ **A** You shouldn't travel in this lane
- ☐ **B** The hard shoulder can be used as a running lane
- ☐ **C** You can park on the hard shoulder if you feel tired
- ☐ **D** You can pull up in this lane to answer a mobile phone

A mandatory speed-limit sign above the hard shoulder shows that this part of the road can be used as a running lane between junctions. You must stay within the speed limit. Look out for vehicles that may have broken down and could be blocking the hard shoulder.

418 Mark *one* answer
What's the aim of a smart motorway?

- ☐ **A** To prevent overtaking
- ☐ **B** To reduce rest stops
- ☐ **C** To prevent tailgating
- ☐ **D** To reduce congestion

Smart motorway schemes are intended to reduce congestion and make journey times more reliable. In these areas, the hard shoulder may be used as a running lane to ease congestion at peak times or in the event of an incident. Variable speed limits are used to help keep the traffic moving and to avoid bunching.

419 Mark *one* answer
You're using a smart motorway. What happens when it's operating?

- ☐ **A** Speed limits above lanes are advisory
- ☐ **B** The national speed limit will apply
- ☐ **C** The speed limit is always 30 mph
- ☐ **D** You must obey the speed limits shown

When a smart motorway is operating, you must follow the mandatory signs on the gantries above each lane, including the hard shoulder. Variable speed limits help keep the traffic moving and also help to prevent bunching.

420 Mark *one* answer
Why can it be an advantage for traffic speed to stay constant over a longer distance?

- ☐ **A** You'll do more stop–start driving
- ☐ **B** You'll use far more fuel
- ☐ **C** You'll be able to use more direct routes
- ☐ **D** Your overall journey time will normally improve

When traffic travels at a constant speed over a longer distance, journey times normally improve. You may feel that you could travel faster for short periods, but this generally leads to bunching and increased overall journey time.

421 Mark *one* answer

You shouldn't normally travel on the hard shoulder of a motorway. When can you use it?

- ☐ **A** When taking the next exit
- ☐ **B** When traffic is stopped
- ☐ **C** When signs direct you to
- ☐ **D** When traffic is slow moving

Normally, you should only use the hard shoulder for emergencies and breakdowns, and at roadworks when signs direct you to do so. Smart motorways use active traffic management to ease congestion. In these areas, the hard shoulder may be used as a running lane when speed-limit signs are shown directly above.

422 Mark *one* answer

What's used to reduce traffic bunching on a motorway?

- ☐ **A** Variable speed limits
- ☐ **B** Contraflow systems
- ☐ **C** National speed limits
- ☐ **D** Lane closures

Congestion can be reduced by keeping traffic at a constant speed. At busy times, maximum speed limits are displayed on overhead gantries. These can be varied quickly, depending on the amount of traffic. By keeping to a constant speed on busy sections of motorway, overall journey times are normally improved.

423 Mark *one* answer

When may you stop on a motorway?

- ☐ **A** If you have to read a map
- ☐ **B** When you're tired and need a rest
- ☐ **C** If your mobile phone rings
- ☐ **D** In an emergency or breakdown

You shouldn't normally stop on a motorway, but there may be occasions when you need to do so. If you're unfortunate enough to break down, make every effort to pull up on the hard shoulder.

424 Mark *one* answer

Unless signs show otherwise, what's the national speed limit for a car or motorcycle on a motorway?

- ☐ **A** 50 mph
- ☐ **B** 60 mph
- ☐ **C** 70 mph
- ☐ **D** 80 mph

The national speed limit for a car or motorcycle on a motorway is 70 mph. Lower speed limits may be in force; for example, at roadworks. Variable speed limits also operate in some areas when the motorway is very busy. Cars or motorcycles towing trailers are subject to a lower speed limit.

425 Mark *one* answer

You stop on the hard shoulder of a motorway and use the emergency telephone. Where's the best place to wait for help to arrive?

□ **A** Next to the phone
□ **B** Well away from the carriageway
□ **C** With your vehicle
□ **D** On the hard shoulder

When you're on the hard shoulder, you're at risk of being injured by motorway traffic. The safest place to wait is away from the carriageway, but near enough to see the emergency services arriving.

---

426 Mark *one* answer

You're on a motorway and there are red flashing lights above every lane. What must you do?

□ **A** Pull onto the hard shoulder
□ **B** Slow down and watch for further signals
□ **C** Leave at the next exit
□ **D** Stop and wait

Red flashing lights above all lanes mean you must stop and wait. You'll also see a red cross lit up. Don't change lanes, don't continue and don't pull onto the hard shoulder (unless in an emergency).

427 Mark *one* answer

You're on a three-lane motorway. A red cross is showing above the hard shoulder and mandatory speed limits above all other lanes. What does this mean?

□ **A** The hard shoulder can be used as a rest area if you feel tired
□ **B** The hard shoulder is for emergency or breakdown use only
□ **C** The hard shoulder can be used as a normal running lane
□ **D** The hard shoulder has a speed limit of 50 mph

A red cross above the hard shoulder shows that it's closed as a running lane and should only be used for emergencies or breakdowns. On a smart motorway, the hard shoulder may be used as a running lane at busy times. This will be shown by a mandatory speed limit on the gantry above the hard shoulder.

428 Mark *one* answer
On a three-lane motorway, what does this sign mean?

☐ **A** Use any lane except the hard shoulder
☐ **B** Use the hard shoulder only
☐ **C** Use the three right-hand lanes only
☐ **D** Use all the lanes, including the hard shoulder

You must obey mandatory speed-limit signs above motorway lanes, including the hard shoulder. In this case, you can use the hard shoulder as a running lane but you should look for any vehicles that may have broken down and may be blocking the hard shoulder.

429 Mark *one* answer
You're travelling along a motorway and feel tired. Where should you stop to rest?

☐ **A** On the hard shoulder
☐ **B** At the nearest service area
☐ **C** On a slip road
☐ **D** On the central reservation

If you feel tired, stop at the nearest service area. If that's too far away, leave the motorway at the next exit and find a safe place to stop. You mustn't stop on the carriageway or hard shoulder of a motorway except in an emergency, when in a traffic queue, or when signalled to do so by a police officer, a traffic officer or traffic signals. Plan your journey so that you have regular rest stops.

430 Mark *one* answer
You're riding slowly in a town centre. Why should you glance over your left shoulder before turning left?

- ☐ **A** To check for cyclists
- ☐ **B** To help keep your balance
- ☐ **C** To look for traffic signs
- ☐ **D** To check for potholes

When riding slowly, you must remember to look out for cyclists – they can travel quickly and fit through surprisingly narrow spaces. Before you turn left in slow-moving traffic, it's important to check that a cyclist isn't trying to filter past on your left.

431 Mark *one* answer
Which lane mustn't you use when you're riding your motorcycle?

- ☐ **A** Crawler lane
- ☐ **B** Overtaking lane
- ☐ **C** Acceleration lane
- ☐ **D** Tram lane

Always plan ahead and be aware of lanes and areas designated for specific road users only. The restrictions are sometimes in force only at certain times of day, and signs will show when they apply. In some towns, motorcycles are permitted to use bus lanes – check the signs carefully.

432 Mark *one* answer
What does this sign mean?

- ☐ **A** No parking for solo motorcycles
- ☐ **B** Parking for solo motorcycles
- ☐ **C** Passing place for motorcycles
- ☐ **D** Police motorcycles only

In some towns and cities there are special areas reserved for parking motorcycles. Look out for these signs.

433 Mark *one* answer
You're riding on a busy dual carriageway. What should you do before you change lanes?

- ☐ **A** Rely totally on your mirrors
- ☐ **B** Always increase your speed
- ☐ **C** Signal so that others will give way
- ☐ **D** Use mirrors and shoulder checks

Before changing direction, as well as using your mirrors, you may need to take a quick sideways glance to check for vehicles in your blind spots. These are the areas behind and to the side of you that aren't covered by your mirrors.

434 Mark *one* answer

You're looking for somewhere to park your motorcycle. The area is full except for spaces marked 'disabled use'. What can you do?

☐ **A** You can use these spaces when elsewhere is full

☐ **B** You can park in one of these spaces if you stay with your motorcycle

☐ **C** You can use one of the spaces as long as one is kept free

☐ **D** You can't park there, unless you're permitted to do so

It's illegal to park in a space reserved for disabled users unless you're permitted to do so. These spaces are provided for people with limited mobility, who may need extra space to get into and out of their vehicle.

435 Mark *one* answer

You're on a road with passing places. It's only wide enough for one vehicle. A car is coming towards you. What should you do?

☐ **A** Pull into a passing place on your right

☐ **B** Force the other driver to reverse

☐ **C** Turn round and ride back to the main road

☐ **D** Pull into a passing place on your left

If you meet another vehicle on a narrow road and the passing place is on your left, pull into it. If the passing place is on your right, wait opposite it.

436 Mark *one* answer

You're both turning right at this crossroads. Why is it safer to keep the car to your right?

☐ **A** So you can see approaching traffic

☐ **B** So you can keep close to the kerb

☐ **C** So you can keep clear of following traffic

☐ **D** So you can make oncoming vehicles stop

When turning right at this crossroads, you should keep the oncoming car to your right. This will give you a clear view of the road ahead and any oncoming traffic.

437 Mark *one* answer

What should you do when filtering through slow-moving or stationary traffic?

☐ **A** Watch for vehicles emerging from side roads

☐ **B** Continually use your horn as a warning

☐ **C** Stand up on the footrests for a good view ahead

☐ **D** Ride with your hazard warning lights on

Other road users may not expect or look for motorcycles filtering through slow-moving or stationary traffic. Your view will be reduced by the vehicles around you. Watch out for pedestrians walking between the vehicles, vehicles suddenly changing direction and vehicles turning into or out of side roads.

438 Mark *one* answer

You're riding towards roadworks. The temporary traffic lights are on red. The road ahead is clear. What should you do?

☐ **A** Ride on with extreme caution
☐ **B** Ride on at normal speed
☐ **C** Carry on if approaching cars have stopped
☐ **D** Wait for the green light

You must obey all traffic signs and signals. Just because the lights are temporary, it doesn't mean that you can disregard them.

439 Mark *one* answer

You intend to go abroad and will be riding on the right-hand side of the road. What should you fit to your motorcycle?

☐ **A** Twin headlights
☐ **B** Headlight deflectors
☐ **C** Tinted yellow brake lights
☐ **D** Tinted red indicator lenses

When abroad and riding on the right, deflectors are usually required to prevent your headlights from dazzling approaching drivers.

440 Mark *one* answer

You want to tow a trailer with your motorcycle. What's the minimum engine size required to do this?

☐ **A** 50 cc
☐ **B** 125 cc
☐ **C** 525 cc
☐ **D** 1000 cc

Towing a trailer requires special care. You must obey the restrictions that apply when towing – including the 125 cc minimum size of your motorcycle engine and the reduced national speed limits. Don't forget the trailer is there, especially when negotiating bends and junctions.

441 Mark *one* answer

What's the national speed limit on a single carriageway?

☐ **A** 40 mph
☐ **B** 50 mph
☐ **C** 60 mph
☐ **D** 70 mph

You don't have to ride at the speed limit. Use your own judgement and ride at a speed that suits the prevailing road, weather and traffic conditions.

442 Mark *one* answer
When must you stop your motorcycle?

- ☐ **A** At a clear pelican crossing when the amber light is flashing
- ☐ **B** At an empty zebra crossing
- ☐ **C** When signalled to do so by a police officer
- ☐ **D** At a junction with double broken white lines

Don't stop or hold up traffic unnecessarily. However, there are occasions when you must stop by law. These include

- when signalled to do so by a school crossing patrol, police officer or traffic officer
- at a red traffic light
- at a junction with a 'stop' sign.

443 Mark *one* answer
What's the meaning of this sign?

- ☐ **A** Local speed limit applies
- ☐ **B** No waiting on the carriageway
- ☐ **C** National speed limit applies
- ☐ **D** No entry for vehicles

This sign doesn't tell you the speed limit in figures. You should know the speed limit for the type of road that you're on and the type of vehicle that you're driving. Study your copy of *The Highway Code*.

444 Mark *one* answer
What's the national speed limit for cars and motorcycles on a dual carriageway?

- ☐ **A** 30 mph
- ☐ **B** 50 mph
- ☐ **C** 60 mph
- ☐ **D** 70 mph

Make sure that you know the speed limit for the road that you're on. The speed limit on a dual carriageway or motorway is 70 mph for cars and motorcycles, unless signs indicate otherwise. The speed limits for different types of vehicle are listed in *The Highway Code*.

445 Mark *one* answer
There are no speed-limit signs on the road. How is a 30 mph limit indicated?

- ☐ **A** By hazard warning lines
- ☐ **B** By street lighting
- ☐ **C** By pedestrian islands
- ☐ **D** By double or single yellow lines

There's a 30 mph speed limit where there are street lights unless signs show another limit.

446 Mark *one* answer

You see street lights but no speed-limit signs. What will the speed limit usually be?

☐ **A** 30 mph
☐ **B** 40 mph
☐ **C** 50 mph
☐ **D** 60 mph

The presence of street lights generally indicates that there's a 30 mph speed limit, unless signs tell you otherwise.

---

447 Mark *one* answer

What does this sign mean?

☐ **A** Minimum speed 30 mph
☐ **B** End of maximum speed
☐ **C** End of minimum speed
☐ **D** Maximum speed 30 mph

The red slash through the sign indicates that the restriction has ended. In this case, the restriction was a minimum speed limit of 30 mph.

448 Mark *one* answer

There's a tractor ahead. You want to overtake but you aren't sure whether it's safe. What should you do?

☐ **A** Follow another vehicle as it overtakes the tractor
☐ **B** Sound your horn to make the tractor pull over
☐ **C** Speed past, flashing your lights at oncoming traffic
☐ **D** Stay behind the tractor if you're in any doubt

Following a tractor can be frustrating, but never overtake if you're unsure whether it's safe. Ask yourself: 'Can I see far enough down the road to ensure that I can complete the manoeuvre safely?' It's better to be delayed for a minute or two than to take a chance that may cause a collision.

---

449 Mark *one* answer

Which vehicle is most likely to take an unusual course at a roundabout?

☐ **A** Estate car
☐ **B** Milk float
☐ **C** Delivery van
☐ **D** Long lorry

Long vehicles might have to take a slightly different position when approaching the roundabout or going around it. This is to stop the rear of the vehicle cutting in and mounting the kerb.

450 Mark *one* answer
When mustn't you stop on a clearway?

- ☐ **A** At any time
- ☐ **B** When it's busy
- ☐ **C** In the rush hour
- ☐ **D** During daylight hours

Clearways are in place so that traffic can flow without the obstruction of parked vehicles. Just one parked vehicle can cause an obstruction for all other traffic. You mustn't stop where a clearway is in force, not even to pick up or set down passengers.

451 Mark *one* answer
What's the meaning of this sign?

- ☐ **A** No entry
- ☐ **B** Waiting restrictions
- ☐ **C** National speed limit
- ☐ **D** School crossing patrol

This sign indicates that there are waiting restrictions. It's normally accompanied by details of when the restrictions are in force.

Details of most signs in common use are shown in *The Highway Code*. For more comprehensive coverage, see *Know Your Road Signs*.

452 Mark *one* answer
When can you park on the right-hand side of a road at night?

- ☐ **A** When you're in a one-way street
- ☐ **B** When you have your sidelights on
- ☐ **C** When you're more than 10 metres (32 feet) from a junction
- ☐ **D** When you're under a lamppost

Red rear reflectors show up when headlights shine on them. These are useful when you're parked at night, but they'll only reflect if you park in the same direction as the traffic flow. Normally you should park on the left, but in a one-way street you may also park on the right-hand side.

453 Mark *one* answer
On a three-lane dual carriageway, what can the right-hand lane be used for?

- ☐ **A** Overtaking only, never turning right
- ☐ **B** Overtaking or turning right
- ☐ **C** Fast-moving traffic only
- ☐ **D** Turning right only, never overtaking

You should normally use the left-hand lane on any dual carriageway unless you're overtaking or turning right.

When overtaking on a dual carriageway, look for vehicles ahead that are turning right. They may be slowing or stopped. You need to see them in good time so that you can take appropriate action.

454 Mark *one* answer

You're approaching a busy junction. What should you do when, at the last moment, you realise you're in the wrong lane?

- ☐ **A** Continue in that lane
- ☐ **B** Force your way across
- ☐ **C** Stop until the area has cleared
- ☐ **D** Use clear arm signals to cut across

There are times when road markings are obscured by queuing traffic, or you're unsure which lane to use. If, at the last moment, you find you're in the wrong lane, don't cut across or bully other drivers to let you in. Follow the lane you're in and find somewhere safe to turn around and rejoin your route.

455 Mark *one* answer

Where may you overtake on a one-way street?

- ☐ **A** Only on the left-hand side
- ☐ **B** Overtaking isn't allowed
- ☐ **C** Only on the right-hand side
- ☐ **D** On either the right or the left

You can overtake other traffic on either side when travelling in a one-way street. Make full use of your mirrors and ensure it's clear all around before you attempt to overtake. Look for signs and road markings, and use the most suitable lane for your destination.

456 Mark *one* answer

How should you signal when going straight ahead at a roundabout?

- ☐ **A** Indicate left before leaving the roundabout
- ☐ **B** Don't indicate at any time
- ☐ **C** Indicate right when approaching the roundabout
- ☐ **D** Indicate left when approaching the roundabout

When going straight ahead at a roundabout, don't signal as you approach it. Indicate left just after passing the exit before the one you wish to take.

457 Mark *one* answer

Which vehicle might have to take a different course from normal at roundabouts?

- ☐ **A** Sports car
- ☐ **B** Van
- ☐ **C** Estate car
- ☐ **D** Long vehicle

A long vehicle may have to straddle lanes either on or approaching a roundabout so that the rear wheels don't hit the kerb.

If you're following a long vehicle, stay well back and give it plenty of room.

458 Mark *one* answer
On which occasion may you enter a box junction?

☐ **A** When there are fewer than two vehicles ahead
☐ **B** When signalled by another road user
☐ **C** When your exit road is clear
☐ **D** When traffic signs direct you

Yellow box junctions are marked on the road to prevent the road becoming blocked. Don't enter the box unless your exit road is clear. You may wait in the box if you want to turn right and your exit road is clear but oncoming traffic or other vehicles waiting to turn right are preventing you from making the turn.

459 Mark *one* answer
When may you stop and wait in a box junction?

☐ **A** When oncoming traffic prevents you from turning right
☐ **B** When you're in a queue of traffic turning left
☐ **C** When you're in a queue of traffic going ahead
☐ **D** When you're on a roundabout

The purpose of yellow box markings is to keep junctions clear of queuing traffic. You may only wait in the marked area when you're turning right and your exit lane is clear but you can't complete the turn because of oncoming traffic or other traffic waiting to turning right.

460 Mark *one* answer
Which person's signal to stop must you obey?

☐ **A** A motorcyclist
☐ **B** A pedestrian
☐ **C** A police officer
☐ **D** A bus driver

You must obey signals to stop given by police and traffic officers, traffic wardens and school crossing patrols. Failure to do so is an offence and could lead to prosecution.

461 Mark *one* answer
You see a pedestrian waiting at a zebra crossing. What should you normally do?

- ☐ **A** Go on quickly before they step onto the crossing
- ☐ **B** Stop before you reach the zigzag lines and let them cross
- ☐ **C** Stop to let them cross and wait patiently
- ☐ **D** Ignore them as they're still on the pavement

By standing on the pavement, the pedestrian is showing an intention to cross. By looking well ahead, you'll give yourself time to see the pedestrian, check your mirrors and respond safely.

462 Mark *one* answer
Who can use a toucan crossing?

- ☐ **A** Cars and motorcycles
- ☐ **B** Cyclists and pedestrians
- ☐ **C** Buses and lorries
- ☐ **D** Trams and trains

Toucan crossings are similar to pelican crossings but there's no flashing amber phase. Cyclists share the crossing with pedestrians and are allowed to cycle across when the green cycle symbol is shown.

463 Mark *one* answer
You're waiting at a pelican crossing. What does it mean when the red light changes to flashing amber?

- ☐ **A** Wait for pedestrians on the crossing to clear
- ☐ **B** Move off immediately without any hesitation
- ☐ **C** Wait for the green light before moving off
- ☐ **D** Get ready and go when the continuous amber light shows

This light allows pedestrians already on the crossing to get to the other side in their own time, without being rushed. Don't rev your engine or start to move off while they're still crossing.

464 Mark *one* answer
When can you park on the left opposite these road markings?

- ☐ **A** If the line nearest to you is broken
- ☐ **B** When there are no yellow lines
- ☐ **C** To pick up or set down passengers
- ☐ **D** During daylight hours only

You mustn't park or stop on a road marked with double white lines (even where one of the lines is broken) except to pick up or set down passengers.

465 Mark *one* answer

You're turning right at a crossroads. An oncoming driver is also turning right. What's the advantage of turning behind the oncoming vehicle?

- ☐ **A** You'll have a clearer view of any approaching traffic
- ☐ **B** You'll use less fuel because you can stay in a higher gear
- ☐ **C** You'll have more time to turn
- ☐ **D** You'll be able to turn without stopping

When turning right at a crossroads where oncoming traffic is also turning right, it's generally safer to turn behind the approaching vehicle. This allows you a clear view of approaching traffic and is called 'turning offside to offside'. However, some junctions, usually controlled by traffic-light filters – are marked for vehicles to turn nearside to nearside.

466 Mark *one* answer

You're travelling along a street with parked vehicles on the left-hand side. Why should you keep your speed down?

- ☐ **A** So that oncoming traffic can see you more clearly
- ☐ **B** You may set off car alarms
- ☐ **C** There may be delivery lorries on the street
- ☐ **D** Children may run out from between the vehicles

Travel slowly and carefully near parked vehicles. Beware of
- vehicles pulling out, especially bicycles and motorcycles
- pedestrians, especially children, who may run out from between cars
- drivers opening their doors.

467 Mark *one* answer

What should you do when you meet an obstruction on your side of the road?

- ☐ **A** Carry on, as you have priority
- ☐ **B** Give way to oncoming traffic
- ☐ **C** Wave oncoming vehicles through
- ☐ **D** Accelerate to get past first

Take care if you have to pass a parked vehicle on your side of the road. Give way to oncoming traffic if there isn't enough room for you both to continue safely.

468 Mark *one* answer

You're on a two-lane dual carriageway. Why would you use the right-hand lane?

- ☐ **A** To overtake slower traffic
- ☐ **B** For normal progress
- ☐ **C** When staying at the minimum allowed speed
- ☐ **D** To keep driving at a constant high speed

Normally you should travel in the left-hand lane and only use the right-hand lane for overtaking or turning right. Move back into the left lane as soon as it's safe but don't cut in across the path of the vehicle you've just passed.

469 Mark *one* answer
Who has priority at an unmarked crossroads?

- ☐ **A** The larger vehicle
- ☐ **B** No-one has priority
- ☐ **C** The faster vehicle
- ☐ **D** The smaller vehicle

Practise good observation in all directions before you emerge or make a turn. Proceed only when you're sure it's safe to do so.

470 Mark *one* answer **NI**
What's the nearest you may park to a junction?

- ☐ **A** 10 metres (32 feet)
- ☐ **B** 12 metres (39 feet)
- ☐ **C** 15 metres (49 feet)
- ☐ **D** 20 metres (66 feet)

Don't park within 10 metres (32 feet) of a junction (unless in an authorised parking place). This is to allow drivers emerging from, or turning into, the junction a clear view of the road they're joining. It also allows them to see hazards such as pedestrians or cyclists at the junction.

471 Mark *one* answer **NI**
Where shouldn't you park?

- ☐ **A** On a road with a 40 mph speed limit
- ☐ **B** At or near a bus stop
- ☐ **C** Where there's no pavement
- ☐ **D** Within 20 metres (65 feet) of a junction

It may be tempting to park where you shouldn't while you run a quick errand. Careless parking is a selfish act and could endanger other road users. It's important not to park at or near a bus stop, as this could inconvenience passengers and may put them at risk as they get on or off the bus.

472 Mark *one* answer
You're waiting at a level crossing. A train passes but the lights keep flashing. What must you do?

- ☐ **A** Carry on waiting
- ☐ **B** Phone the signal operator
- ☐ **C** Edge over the stop line and look for trains
- ☐ **D** Park and investigate

If the lights at a level crossing keep flashing after a train has passed, you should continue to wait, because another train might be coming. Time seems to pass slowly when you're held up in a queue. Be patient and wait until the lights stop flashing.

473 Mark *one* answer
What does this sign tell you?

☐ **A** No through road
☐ **B** End of traffic-calming zone
☐ **C** Free-parking zone ends
☐ **D** No-waiting zone ends

The blue-and-red circular sign on its own means that waiting restrictions are in force. This sign shows that you're leaving the controlled zone and waiting restrictions no longer apply.

474 Mark *one* answer
What must you do when entering roadworks where a temporary speed limit is displayed?

☐ **A** Obey the speed limit
☐ **B** Obey the limit, but only during rush hour
☐ **C** Ignore the displayed limit
☐ **D** Use your own judgment; the limit is only advisory

Where there are extra hazards, such as at roadworks, it's often necessary to slow traffic down by imposing a lower speed limit. These speed limits aren't advisory; they must be obeyed.

475 Mark *one* answer
You're on a well-lit road at night, in a built-up area. How will using dipped headlights help?

☐ **A** You can see further along the road
☐ **B** You can go at a much faster speed
☐ **C** You can switch to main beam quickly
☐ **D** You can be easily seen by others

You may be difficult to see when you're travelling at night, even on a well-lit road. If you use dipped headlights rather than sidelights, other road users should be able to see you more easily.

476 Mark *one* answer
The dual carriageway you're turning right onto has a very narrow central reservation. What should you do?

☐ **A** Proceed to the central reservation and wait
☐ **B** Wait until the road is clear in both directions
☐ **C** Stop in the first lane so that other vehicles give way
☐ **D** Emerge slightly to show your intentions

When the central reservation is narrow, you should treat a dual carriageway as one road. Wait until the road is clear in both directions before emerging to turn right. If you try to treat it as two separate roads and wait in the middle, you're likely to cause an obstruction and possibly a collision.

477 Mark *one* answer

What's the national speed limit on a single carriageway road for cars and motorcycles?

☐ **A** 30 mph
☐ **B** 50 mph
☐ **C** 60 mph
☐ **D** 70 mph

Exceeding the speed limit is dangerous and can result in you receiving penalty points on your licence. It isn't worth it. You should know the speed limit for the road that you're on by observing the road signs. Different speed limits apply if you're towing a trailer.

478 Mark *one* answer

You park at night on a road with a 40 mph speed limit. What should you do?

☐ **A** Park facing the traffic
☐ **B** Park with parking lights on
☐ **C** Park with dipped headlights on
☐ **D** Park near a street light

You must use parking lights when parking at night on a road or in a lay-by on a road with a speed limit greater than 30 mph. You must also park in the direction of the traffic flow and not close to a junction.

479 Mark *one* answer

Where will you see these red and white markers?

☐ **A** Approaching the end of a motorway
☐ **B** Approaching a concealed level crossing
☐ **C** Approaching a concealed speed-limit sign
☐ **D** Approaching the end of a dual carriageway

If there's a bend just before a level crossing, you may not be able to see the level-crossing barriers or waiting traffic. These signs give you an early warning that you may find these hazards just around the bend.

480 Mark *one* answer

You're travelling on a motorway in England. You must stop when signalled to do so by which of these?

- ☐ **A** Flashing amber lights above your lane
- ☐ **B** A traffic officer
- ☐ **C** Pedestrians on the hard shoulder
- ☐ **D** A driver who has broken down

You'll find traffic officers on England's motorways. They work in partnership with the police, helping to keep traffic moving and helping to make your journey as safe as possible. It's an offence not to comply with the directions given by a traffic officer.

481 Mark *one* answer

You're going straight ahead at a roundabout. How should you signal?

- ☐ **A** Signal right on the approach and then left to leave the roundabout
- ☐ **B** Signal left after you leave the roundabout and enter the new road
- ☐ **C** Signal right on the approach to the roundabout and keep the signal on
- ☐ **D** Signal left just after you pass the exit before the one you're going to take

To go straight ahead at a roundabout, you should normally approach in the left-hand lane, but check the road markings. At some roundabouts, the left lane on approach is marked 'left turn only', so make sure you use the correct lane to go ahead. You won't normally need to signal as you approach, but signal before you leave the roundabout, as other road users need to know your intentions.

482 Mark *one* answer

How should you give an arm signal to turn left?

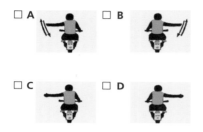

Arm signals can be effective during daylight, especially when you're wearing bright clothing. Practise giving arm signals when you're learning. You need to be able to keep full control of your motorcycle with one hand off the handlebars.

483 Mark *one* answer

You're giving an arm signal, ready to turn left. Why shouldn't you continue with the arm signal while you turn?

☐ **A** Because you might hit a pedestrian on the corner
☐ **B** Because you'll have less steering control
☐ **C** Because you'll need to keep the clutch applied
☐ **D** Because other motorists will think that you're stopping on the corner

Consider giving an arm signal if it will help other road users; for example, in bright sunshine, when your indicators may be difficult to see. Don't maintain an arm signal when turning, but return your hand to the handlebars to help you steer through the turn.

484 Mark *one* answer
What does this sign mean?

- ☐ **A** Side winds
- ☐ **B** Airport
- ☐ **C** Slippery road
- ☐ **D** Service area

Strong side winds can suddenly blow you off course. Keep your speed down when it's very windy, especially on exposed roads.

485 Mark *one* answer
Which of these signs are you allowed to ride past on a solo motorcycle?

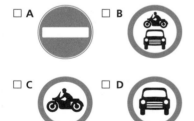

Most regulatory signs are circular. A red circle tells you what you mustn't do.

486 Mark *one* answer
Which of these signals should you give when slowing or stopping your motorcycle?

Arm signals can be given to reinforce your flashing indicators, especially if the indicator signal could cause confusion; for example, if you intend to pull up close to a side road.

487 Mark *one* answer
Why should you make sure that you cancel your indicators after turning?

- ☐ **A** To avoid flattening the battery
- ☐ **B** To avoid misleading other road users
- ☐ **C** To avoid dazzling other road users
- ☐ **D** To avoid damage to the indicator relay

Always check that you've cancelled your indicators after turning. Failing to cancel your indicators could lead to a serious or even fatal collision. Other road users might pull out in front of you if they think you're going to turn off before you reach them.

488 Mark *one* answer

Your indicators are difficult to see due to bright sunshine. What should you do to let other road users know your intentions?

- ☐ **A** Give an arm signal
- ☐ **B** Sound your horn
- ☐ **C** Flash your headlights
- ☐ **D** Keep both hands on the handlebars

Arm signals should be used to confirm your intentions when you aren't sure that your indicators can be seen by other road users. Use the signals shown in *The Highway Code* and return your hand to the handlebars before you turn.

489 Mark *one* answer

You're riding on a motorway. There's a slow-moving vehicle ahead. On the back, you see this sign. What should you do?

- ☐ **A** Pass on the right
- ☐ **B** Pass on the left
- ☐ **C** Leave at the next exit
- ☐ **D** Drive no further

If this vehicle is in your lane, you'll have to move to the left. Use your mirrors and signal if necessary. When it's safe, move into the lane on your left. You should always look well ahead so that you can spot such hazards early, giving yourself time to react safely.

490 Mark *one* answer

How can you identify traffic signs that give orders?

- ☐ **A** They're rectangular with a yellow border
- ☐ **B** They're triangular with a blue border
- ☐ **C** They're square with a brown border
- ☐ **D** They're circular with a red border

There are three basic types of traffic sign: those that warn, those that inform and those that give orders. Generally, triangular signs warn, rectangular signs give information or directions and circular signs give orders. An exception is the eight-sided 'stop' sign.

491 Mark *one* answer

Traffic signs giving orders are generally which shape?

Road signs in the shape of a circle give orders. Those with a red circle are mostly prohibitive. The 'stop' sign is octagonal to give it greater prominence. Signs giving orders must always be obeyed.

492 Mark *one* answer
Which type of sign tells you not to do something?

☐ A ☐ B

☐ C ☐ D

Signs in the shape of a circle give orders. A sign with a red circle means that you aren't allowed to do something. Study *Know Your Road Signs* to ensure that you understand what the different traffic signs mean.

493 Mark *one* answer
What does this sign mean?

☐ **A** Maximum speed limit with traffic calming
☐ **B** Minimum speed limit with traffic calming
☐ **C** '20 cars only' parking zone
☐ **D** Only 20 cars allowed at any one time

If you're in a place where there are likely to be pedestrians (for example, outside a school, near a park, in a residential area or in a shopping area), you should be cautious and keep your speed down.

Many local authorities have taken steps to slow traffic down by creating traffic-calming measures such as speed humps. They're there for a reason; slow down.

494 Mark *one* answer
Which sign means no motor vehicles are allowed?

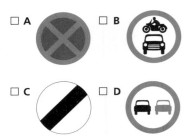

☐ A ☐ B

☐ C ☐ D

You'll generally see this sign at the approach to a pedestrian-only zone.

495 Mark *one* answer
What does this sign mean?

☐ **A** New speed limit 20 mph
☐ **B** No vehicles over 30 tonnes
☐ **C** Minimum speed limit 30 mph
☐ **D** End of 20 mph zone

Where you see this sign, the 20 mph restriction ends. Check all around for possible hazards and only increase your speed if it's safe to do so.

496 Mark *one* answer
What does this sign mean?

- ☐ **A** No overtaking
- ☐ **B** No motor vehicles
- ☐ **C** Clearway (no stopping)
- ☐ **D** Cars and motorcycles only

A sign will indicate which types of vehicles are prohibited from certain roads. Make sure that you know which signs apply to the vehicle you're using.

497 Mark *one* answer
What does this sign mean?

- ☐ **A** No parking
- ☐ **B** No road markings
- ☐ **C** No through road
- ☐ **D** No entry

'No entry' signs are used in places such as one-way streets to prevent vehicles driving against the traffic. To ignore one would be dangerous, both for yourself and for other road users, as well as being against the law.

498 Mark *one* answer
What does this sign mean?

- ☐ **A** Bend to the right
- ☐ **B** Road on the right closed
- ☐ **C** No traffic from the right
- ☐ **D** No right turn

The 'no right turn' sign may be used to warn road users that there's a 'no entry' prohibition on a road to the right ahead.

499 Mark *one* answer
Which sign means 'no entry'?

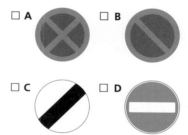

- ☐ **A**
- ☐ **B**
- ☐ **C**
- ☐ **D**

Look for and obey traffic signs. Disobeying or not seeing a sign could be dangerous. It may also be an offence for which you could be prosecuted.

500 Mark *one* answer
What does this sign mean?

- ☐ **A** Route for trams only
- ☐ **B** Route for buses only
- ☐ **C** Parking for buses only
- ☐ **D** Parking for trams only

Avoid blocking tram routes. Trams are fixed on their route and can't manoeuvre around other vehicles or pedestrians. Modern trams travel quickly and are quiet, so you might not hear them approaching.

501 Mark *one* answer
Which type of vehicle does this sign apply to?

- ☐ **A** Wide vehicles
- ☐ **B** Long vehicles
- ☐ **C** High vehicles
- ☐ **D** Heavy vehicles

The triangular shapes above and below the dimensions indicate a height restriction that applies to the road ahead.

502 Mark *one* answer
Which sign means no motor vehicles allowed?

☐ **A**   ☐ **B**

☐ **C**   ☐ **D**

This sign is used to enable pedestrians to walk free from traffic. It's often found in shopping areas.

503 Mark *one* answer
What does this sign mean?

- ☐ **A** You have priority
- ☐ **B** No motor vehicles
- ☐ **C** Two-way traffic
- ☐ **D** No overtaking

Road signs that prohibit overtaking are placed in locations where passing the vehicle in front is dangerous. If you see this sign, don't attempt to overtake. The sign is there for a reason; you must obey it.

504 Mark *one* answer
What does this sign mean?

- ☐ **A** Waiting restrictions apply
- ☐ **B** Waiting permitted
- ☐ **C** National speed limit applies
- ☐ **D** Clearway (no stopping)

There'll be a plate or additional sign to tell you when the restrictions apply.

505 Mark *one* answer
What does this sign mean?

- ☐ **A** End of restricted speed area
- ☐ **B** End of restricted parking area
- ☐ **C** End of clearway
- ☐ **D** End of cycle route

Even though you've left the restricted area, make sure that you park where you won't endanger other road users or cause an obstruction.

506 Mark *one* answer
Which sign means 'no stopping'?

Stopping where this clearway restriction applies is likely to cause congestion. Allow the traffic to flow by obeying the signs.

507 Mark *one* answer
You see this sign ahead. What does it mean?

- ☐ **A** National speed limit applies
- ☐ **B** Waiting restrictions apply
- ☐ **C** No stopping
- ☐ **D** No entry

Clearways are stretches of road where you aren't allowed to stop unless it's an emergency. Stopping where these restrictions apply may be dangerous and is likely to cause an obstruction. Restrictions might apply for several miles and this may be indicated on the sign.

508 Mark *one* answer
What does this sign mean?

☐ **A** Distance to parking place ahead
☐ **B** Distance to public telephone ahead
☐ **C** Distance to public house ahead
☐ **D** Distance to passing place ahead

If you intend to stop and rest, this sign allows you time to reduce speed and pull over safely.

509 Mark *one* answer
What does this sign mean?

☐ **A** Vehicles may not park on the verge or footway
☐ **B** Vehicles may park on the left-hand side of the road only
☐ **C** Vehicles may park fully on the verge or footway
☐ **D** Vehicles may park on the right-hand side of the road only

In order to keep roads free from parked cars, there are some areas where you're allowed to park on the verge. Only do this where you see the sign. Parking on verges or footways anywhere else could lead to a fine.

510 Mark *one* answer
What does this traffic sign mean?

☐ **A** No overtaking allowed
☐ **B** Give priority to oncoming traffic
☐ **C** Two-way traffic
☐ **D** One-way traffic only

Priority signs are normally shown where the road is narrow and there isn't enough room for two vehicles to pass. Examples are narrow bridges, roadworks and where there's a width restriction.

Make sure you know who has priority; don't force your way through. Show courtesy and consideration to other road users.

511 Mark *one* answer
What's the meaning of this traffic sign?

- ☐ **A** End of two-way road
- ☐ **B** Give priority to vehicles coming towards you
- ☐ **C** You have priority over vehicles coming towards you
- ☐ **D** Bus lane ahead

Don't force your way through. Show courtesy and consideration to other road users. Although you have priority, make sure oncoming traffic is going to give way before you continue.

512 Mark *one* answer
What shape is a 'stop' sign at a junction?

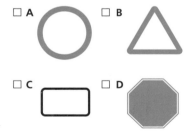

☐ A

☐ B

☐ C

☐ D

To make it easy to recognise, the 'stop' sign is the only sign of this shape. You must stop and take effective observation before proceeding.

513 Mark *one* answer
At a junction, you see this sign partly covered by snow. What does it mean?

- ☐ **A** Crossroads
- ☐ **B** Give way
- ☐ **C** Stop
- ☐ **D** Turn right

The 'stop' sign is the only road sign that's octagonal. This is so that it can be recognised and obeyed even if it's obscured (for example, by snow).

514 Mark *one* answer
What does this sign mean?

- ☐ **A** Service area 30 miles ahead
- ☐ **B** Maximum speed 30 mph
- ☐ **C** Minimum speed 30 mph
- ☐ **D** Lay-by 30 miles ahead

This sign is shown where slow-moving vehicles would impede the flow of traffic; for example, in tunnels. However, if you need to slow down or even stop to avoid an incident or potential collision, you should do so.

515 Mark *one* answer
What does this sign mean?

- ☐ **A** Give way to oncoming vehicles
- ☐ **B** Approaching traffic passes you on both sides
- ☐ **C** Turn off at the next available junction
- ☐ **D** Pass either side to get to the same destination

These signs are often seen in one-way streets that have more than one lane. When you see this sign, use the route that's the most convenient and doesn't require a late change of direction.

516 Mark *one* answer
What does this sign mean?

- ☐ **A** Route for trams
- ☐ **B** Give way to trams
- ☐ **C** Route for buses
- ☐ **D** Give way to buses

Take extra care when you encounter trams. Look out for road markings and signs that alert you to them. Modern trams are very quiet and you may not hear them approaching.

517 Mark *one* answer
What does a circular traffic sign with a blue background do?

- ☐ **A** Give warning of a motorway ahead
- ☐ **B** Give directions to a car park
- ☐ **C** Give motorway information
- ☐ **D** Give an instruction

Signs with blue circles mostly give a positive instruction. These are often found in urban areas and include signs for mini-roundabouts and directional arrows.

518 Mark *one* answer
Where would you see a contraflow bus and cycle lane?

- ☐ **A** On a dual carriageway
- ☐ **B** On a roundabout
- ☐ **C** On an urban motorway
- ☐ **D** On a one-way street

The traffic permitted to use a contraflow lane travels in the opposite direction to traffic in the other lanes on the road.

519 Mark *one* answer
What does this sign mean?

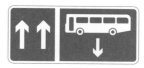

- ☐ **A** Bus station on the right
- ☐ **B** Contraflow bus lane
- ☐ **C** With-flow bus lane
- ☐ **D** Give way to buses

There will also be markings on the road surface to indicate the bus lane. You mustn't use this lane for parking or overtaking.

520 Mark *one* answer
What does a sign with a brown background show?

- ☐ **A** Tourist directions
- ☐ **B** Primary roads
- ☐ **C** Motorway routes
- ☐ **D** Minor roads

Signs with a brown background give directions to places of interest. They're often seen on a motorway, directing you along the easiest route to the attraction.

521 Mark *one* answer
What does this sign mean?

- ☐ **A** Tourist attraction
- ☐ **B** Beware of trains
- ☐ **C** Level crossing
- ☐ **D** Beware of trams

These signs indicate places of interest and are designed to guide you by the easiest route. They're particularly useful when you're unfamiliar with the area.

522 Mark *one* answer
What are triangular signs for?

- ☐ **A** To give warnings
- ☐ **B** To give information
- ☐ **C** To give orders
- ☐ **D** To give directions

This type of sign warns you of hazards ahead. Make sure you look at each sign that you pass on the road, so that you don't miss any vital instructions or information.

523 Mark *one* answer
What does this sign mean?

☐ **A** Turn left ahead
☐ **B** T-junction
☐ **C** No through road
☐ **D** Give way

This type of sign warns you of hazards ahead. Make sure you look at each sign and road marking that you pass, so that you don't miss any vital instructions or information. This particular sign shows there's a T-junction with priority over vehicles from the right.

524 Mark *one* answer
What does this sign mean?

☐ **A** Multi-exit roundabout
☐ **B** Risk of ice
☐ **C** Six roads converge
☐ **D** Place of historical interest

It will take up to ten times longer to stop when it's icy. Where there's a risk of icy conditions, you need to be aware of this and take extra care. If you think the road may be icy, don't brake or steer harshly, as your tyres could lose their grip on the road.

525 Mark *one* answer
What does this sign mean?

☐ **A** Crossroads
☐ **B** Level crossing with gate
☐ **C** Level crossing without gate
☐ **D** Ahead only

The priority through the junction is shown by the broader line. You need to be aware of the hazard posed by traffic crossing or pulling out onto a major road.

526 Mark *one* answer
What does this sign mean?

☐ **A** Ring road
☐ **B** Mini-roundabout
☐ **C** No vehicles
☐ **D** Roundabout

As you approach a roundabout, look well ahead and check all signs. Decide which exit you wish to take and move into the correct position as you approach the roundabout, signalling as required.

527 Mark *one* answer

What information would be shown in a triangular road sign?

- ☐ **A** Road narrows
- ☐ **B** Ahead only
- ☐ **C** Keep left
- ☐ **D** Minimum speed

Warning signs are there to make you aware of potential hazards on the road ahead. Take note of the signs so you're prepared and can take whatever action is necessary.

528 Mark *one* answer

What does this sign mean?

- ☐ **A** Cyclists must dismount
- ☐ **B** Cycles aren't allowed
- ☐ **C** Cycle route ahead
- ☐ **D** Cycle in single file

Where there's a cycle route ahead, a sign will show a bicycle in a red warning triangle. Watch out for children on bicycles and cyclists rejoining the main road.

529 Mark *one* answer

Which sign means that pedestrians may be walking along the road?

☐ **A**   ☐ **B**

☐ **C**   ☐ **D**

When you pass pedestrians in the road, leave plenty of room. You might have to use the right-hand side of the road, so look well ahead, as well as in your mirrors, before pulling out. Take great care if a bend in the road obscures your view ahead.

530 Mark *one* answer

Which of these signs means there's a double bend ahead?

☐ **A**   ☐ **B**

☐ **C**   ☐ **D**

Triangular signs give you a warning of hazards ahead. They're there to give you time to prepare for the hazard; for example, by adjusting your speed.

531 Mark *one* answer
What does this sign mean?

- ☐ **A** Wait at the barriers
- ☐ **B** Wait at the crossroads
- ☐ **C** Give way to trams
- ☐ **D** Give way to farm vehicles

Obey the 'give way' signs. Trams are unable to steer around you if you misjudge when it's safe to enter the junction.

532 Mark *one* answer
What does this sign mean?

- ☐ **A** Hump bridge
- ☐ **B** Humps in the road
- ☐ **C** Entrance to tunnel
- ☐ **D** Soft verges

These humps have been put in place to slow the traffic down. They're usually found in residential areas. Slow down to an appropriate speed.

533 Mark *one* answer
Which of these signs means the end of a dual carriageway?

☐ **A** ☐ **B**

☐ **C** ☐ **D**

If you're overtaking, make sure you move back safely into the left-hand lane before you reach the end of the dual carriageway.

534 Mark *one* answer
What does this sign mean?

- ☐ **A** End of dual carriageway
- ☐ **B** Tall bridge
- ☐ **C** Road narrows
- ☐ **D** End of narrow bridge

Don't wait until the last moment before moving into the left-hand lane. Plan ahead and don't rely on other traffic letting you in.

535 Mark *one* answer
What does this sign mean?

☐ **A** Side winds
☐ **B** Road noise
☐ **C** Airport
☐ **D** Adverse camber

A warning sign with a picture of a windsock indicates that there may be strong side winds. This sign is often found on exposed roads.

536 Mark *one* answer
What does this traffic sign mean?

☐ **A** Slippery road ahead
☐ **B** Tyres liable to punctures ahead
☐ **C** Danger ahead
☐ **D** Service area ahead

This sign is there to alert you to the likelihood of danger ahead. It may be accompanied by a plate indicating the type of hazard. Be ready to reduce your speed and take avoiding action.

537 Mark *one* answer
You're about to overtake. What should you do when you see this sign?

Hidden dip

☐ **A** Overtake the other driver as quickly as possible
☐ **B** Move to the right to get a better view
☐ **C** Switch your headlights on before overtaking
☐ **D** Hold back until you can see clearly ahead

You won't be able to see any hazards that might be hidden in the dip. As well as oncoming traffic, the dip may conceal
  • cyclists
  • horse riders
  • parked vehicles
  • pedestrians in the road.

538 Mark *one* answer
What does this sign mean?

- ☐ **A** Level crossing with gate or barrier
- ☐ **B** Gated road ahead
- ☐ **C** Level crossing without gate or barrier
- ☐ **D** Cattle grid ahead

Some crossings have gates but no attendant or signals. You should stop, look both ways, listen and make sure that no train is approaching. If there's a telephone, contact the signal operator to make sure it's safe to cross.

539 Mark *one* answer
What does this sign mean?

- ☐ **A** No trams ahead
- ☐ **B** Oncoming trams
- ☐ **C** Trams crossing ahead
- ☐ **D** Trams only

This sign tells you to beware of trams. If you don't usually drive in a town where there are trams, remember to look out for them at junctions and look for tram rails, signs and signals.

540 Mark *one* answer
What does this sign mean?

- ☐ **A** Adverse camber
- ☐ **B** Steep hill downwards
- ☐ **C** Uneven road
- ☐ **D** Steep hill upwards

This sign gives you an early warning that the road ahead will slope downhill. Prepare to alter your speed and gear. Looking at the sign from left to right will show you whether the road slopes uphill or downhill.

541 Mark *one* answer
What does this sign mean?

- ☐ **A** Uneven road surface
- ☐ **B** Bridge over the road
- ☐ **C** Road ahead ends
- ☐ **D** Water across the road

This sign is found where a shallow stream crosses the road. Heavy rainfall could increase the flow of water. If the water looks too deep or the stream has spread over a large distance, stop and find another route.

542 Mark *one* answer
What does this sign mean?

- ☐ **A** Turn left for parking area
- ☐ **B** No through road on the left
- ☐ **C** No entry for traffic turning left
- ☐ **D** Turn left for ferry terminal

This sign shows you that you can't get through to another route by turning left at the junction ahead.

543 Mark *one* answer
What does this sign mean?

- ☐ **A** T-junction
- ☐ **B** No through road
- ☐ **C** Telephone box ahead
- ☐ **D** Toilet ahead

You won't be able to find a through route to another road. Use this road only for access.

544 Mark *one* answer
Which sign means 'no through road'?

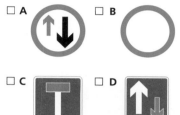

- ☐ **A**
- ☐ **B**
- ☐ **C**
- ☐ **D**

This sign is found at the entrance to a road that can only be used for access.

545 Mark *one* answer
Which is the sign for a ring road?

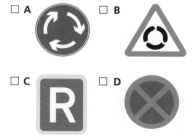

- ☐ **A**
- ☐ **B**
- ☐ **C**
- ☐ **D**

Ring roads are designed to relieve congestion in towns and city centres.

546 Mark *one* answer
What does this sign mean?

- ☐ **A** The right-hand lane ahead is narrow
- ☐ **B** Right-hand lane for buses only
- ☐ **C** Right-hand lane for turning right
- ☐ **D** The right-hand lane is closed

Yellow-and-black temporary signs may be used to inform you about roadworks or lane restrictions. Look well ahead. If you have to change lanes, do so in good time.

547 Mark *one* answer
What does this sign mean?

- ☐ **A** Change to the left lane
- ☐ **B** Leave at the next exit
- ☐ **C** Contraflow system
- ☐ **D** One-way street

If you use the right-hand lane in a contraflow system, you'll be travelling with no permanent barrier between you and the oncoming traffic. Observe speed limits and keep a good distance from the vehicle ahead.

548 Mark *one* answer
What does this sign mean?

- ☐ **A** Leave motorway at next exit
- ☐ **B** Lane for heavy and slow vehicles
- ☐ **C** All lorries use the hard shoulder
- ☐ **D** Rest area for lorries

Where there's a long, steep, uphill gradient on a motorway, a crawler lane may be provided. This helps the traffic to flow by diverting the slower heavy vehicles into a dedicated lane on the left.

549 Mark *one* answer
What does a red traffic light mean?

- ☐ **A** You should stop unless turning left
- ☐ **B** Stop, if you're able to brake safely
- ☐ **C** You must stop and wait behind the stop line
- ☐ **D** Proceed with care

Whatever light is showing, you should know which light is going to appear next and be able to take appropriate action. For example, when amber is showing on its own, you'll know that red will appear next. This should give you ample time to anticipate and respond safely.

550 Mark *one* answer
At traffic lights, what does it mean when the amber light shows on its own?

- ☐ **A** Prepare to go
- ☐ **B** Go if the way is clear
- ☐ **C** Go if no pedestrians are crossing
- ☐ **D** Stop at the stop line

When the amber light is showing on its own, the red light will follow next. The amber light means stop, unless you've already crossed the stop line or you're so close to it that stopping may cause a collision.

551 Mark *one* answer
You're at a junction controlled by traffic lights. When shouldn't you proceed at green?

- ☐ **A** When pedestrians are waiting to cross
- ☐ **B** When your exit from the junction is blocked
- ☐ **C** When you think the lights may be about to change
- ☐ **D** When you intend to turn right

As you approach the lights, look into the road you wish to take. Only proceed if your exit road is clear. If the road is blocked, hold back, even if you have to wait for the next green signal.

552 Mark *one* answer
You're in the left-hand lane at traffic lights, waiting to turn left. At which of these traffic lights mustn't you move on?

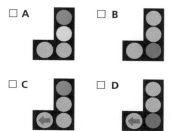

- ☐ **A**
- ☐ **B**
- ☐ **C**
- ☐ **D**

At some junctions, there may be separate signals for different lanes. These are called 'filter' lights. They're designed to help traffic flow at major junctions. Make sure that you're in the correct lane and proceed if the way is clear and the green light shows for your lane.

553 Mark *one* answer
What does this sign mean?

- ☐ **A** Traffic lights out of order
- ☐ **B** Amber signal out of order
- ☐ **C** Temporary traffic lights ahead
- ☐ **D** New traffic lights ahead

You might see this sign where traffic lights are out of order. Proceed with caution, as nobody has priority at the junction.

554 Mark *one* answer
When traffic lights are out of order, who has priority?

☐ **A** Traffic going straight on
☐ **B** Traffic turning right
☐ **C** Nobody
☐ **D** Traffic turning left

When traffic lights are out of order, you should treat the junction as an unmarked crossroads. Be cautious, as you may need to give way or stop. Look for traffic attempting to cross the junction, unaware that it doesn't have priority.

555 Mark *one* answer
These flashing red lights mean that you must stop. Where would you find them?

☐ **A** Pelican crossings
☐ **B** Motorway exits
☐ **C** Zebra crossings
☐ **D** Level crossings

These signals are found at level crossings, swing or lifting bridges, some airfields and emergency access sites. The flashing red lights mean stop whether or not the way seems to be clear.

556 Mark *one* answer
What do these zigzag lines at pedestrian crossings mean?

☐ **A** No parking at any time
☐ **B** Parking allowed only for a short time
☐ **C** Slow down to 20 mph
☐ **D** Sounding horns isn't allowed

The approach to, and exit from, a pedestrian crossing is marked with zigzag lines. You mustn't park on them or overtake the leading vehicle when approaching the crossing. Parking here would block the view for pedestrians and approaching traffic.

557 Mark *one* answer

When may you cross a double solid white line in the middle of the road?

- ☐ **A** To pass traffic that's queuing back at a junction
- ☐ **B** To pass a car signalling to turn left ahead
- ☐ **C** To pass a road maintenance vehicle travelling at 10 mph or less
- ☐ **D** To pass a vehicle that's towing a trailer

You may cross the solid white line to pass a stationary vehicle or to pass a pedal cycle, horse or road maintenance vehicle if it's travelling at 10 mph or less. You may also cross the solid white line to enter a side road or access a property.

558 Mark *one* answer

What does this road marking mean?

- ☐ **A** Don't cross the line
- ☐ **B** No stopping allowed
- ☐ **C** You're approaching a hazard
- ☐ **D** No overtaking allowed

Road markings will warn you of a hazard ahead. A single broken line along the centre of the road, with long markings and short gaps, is a hazard warning line. Don't cross it unless you can see that the road is clear well ahead.

559 Mark *one* answer

Where would you see this road marking?

- ☐ **A** At traffic lights
- ☐ **B** On road humps
- ☐ **C** Near a level crossing
- ☐ **D** At a box junction

Because the road has a dark colour, changes in level aren't easily seen. White triangles painted on the road surface give you an indication of where there are road humps.

560 Mark *one* answer
Which of these is a hazard warning line?

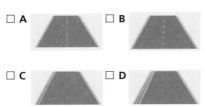

☐ A   ☐ B
☐ C   ☐ D

You need to know the difference between the normal centre line and a hazard warning line. If there's a hazard ahead, the markings are longer and the gaps shorter. This gives you advance warning of an unspecified hazard.

561 Mark *one* answer
At this junction, there's a 'stop' sign and a solid white line on the road surface. Why is there a 'stop' sign here?

☐ **A** Speed on the major road is derestricted
☐ **B** It's a busy junction
☐ **C** Visibility along the major road is restricted
☐ **D** There are hazard warning lines in the centre of the road

If your view at a road junction is restricted, you must stop. There may also be a 'stop' sign. Don't emerge until you're sure no traffic is approaching. If you don't know, don't go.

562 Mark *one* answer
You see this line across the road at the entrance to a roundabout. What does it mean?

☐ **A** Give way to traffic from the right
☐ **B** Traffic from the left has right of way
☐ **C** You have right of way
☐ **D** Stop at the line

Slow down as you approach the roundabout and check for traffic from the right. If you need to stop and give way, stay behind the broken line until it's safe to emerge onto the roundabout.

563 Mark *one* answer
How will a police officer in a patrol vehicle normally get you to stop?

☐ **A** Flash the headlights, indicate left and point to the left
☐ **B** Wait until you stop, then approach you
☐ **C** Use the siren, overtake, cut in front and stop
☐ **D** Pull alongside you, use the siren and wave you to stop

You must obey signals given by the police. If a police officer in a patrol vehicle wants you to pull over, they'll indicate this without causing danger to you or other traffic.

564 Mark *one* answer

You're approaching a junction where the traffic lights aren't working. What should you do when a police officer gives this signal?

- ☐ **A** Turn left only
- ☐ **B** Turn right only
- ☐ **C** Continue ahead only
- ☐ **D** Stop at the stop line

When a police officer or traffic warden is directing traffic, you must obey them. They'll use the arm signals shown in *The Highway Code*. Learn what these signals mean and obey them.

565 Mark *one* answer

The driver of the car in front is giving this arm signal. What does it mean?

- ☐ **A** The driver is slowing down
- ☐ **B** The driver intends to turn right
- ☐ **C** The driver wishes to overtake
- ☐ **D** The driver intends to turn left

There might be an occasion where another driver uses an arm signal. This may be because the vehicle's indicators are obscured by other traffic. In order for such signals to be effective, all drivers should know their meaning. Be aware that the 'left turn' signal might look similar to the 'slowing down' signal.

566 Mark *one* answer

Where would you see these road markings?

- ☐ **A** At a level crossing
- ☐ **B** On a motorway slip road
- ☐ **C** At a pedestrian crossing
- ☐ **D** On a single-track road

When driving on a motorway or slip road, you mustn't enter an area marked with chevrons and bordered by a solid white line for any reason, except in an emergency.

567 Mark *one* answer
What does this motorway sign mean?

- ☐ **A** Change to the lane on your left
- ☐ **B** Leave the motorway at the next exit
- ☐ **C** Change to the opposite carriageway
- ☐ **D** Pull up on the hard shoulder

On the motorway, signs sometimes show temporary warnings due to traffic or weather conditions. They may be used to indicate

- • lane closures
- • temporary speed limits
- • weather warnings.

568 Mark *one* answer
What does this motorway sign mean?

- ☐ **A** Temporary minimum speed 50 mph
- ☐ **B** No services for 50 miles
- ☐ **C** Obstruction 50 metres (164 feet) ahead
- ☐ **D** Temporary maximum speed 50 mph

Look out for signs above your lane or on the central reservation. These will give you important information or warnings about the road ahead. To allow for the high speed of motorway traffic, these signs may light up some distance from any hazard. Don't ignore the signs just because the road looks clear to you.

569 Mark *one* answer
What does this sign mean?

- ☐ **A** Through traffic to use left lane
- ☐ **B** Right-hand lane T-junction only
- ☐ **C** Right-hand lane closed ahead
- ☐ **D** 11 tonne weight limit

You should change lanes as directed by the sign. Here, the right-hand lane is closed but the left-hand and centre lanes are available. Merging in turn is recommended when it's safe and traffic is going slowly; for example, at roadworks or a road traffic incident. When vehicles are travelling at speed, this isn't advisable and you should move into the appropriate lane in good time.

570 Mark *one* answer
What does '25' mean on this motorway sign?

- ☐ **A** The distance to the nearest town
- ☐ **B** The route number of the road
- ☐ **C** The number of the next junction
- ☐ **D** The speed limit on the slip road

Before you set out on your journey, use a road map to plan your route. When you see an advance warning of your junction, make sure you get into the correct lane in plenty of time. Last-minute harsh braking and cutting across lanes at speed is extremely hazardous.

571 Mark *one* answer
How should the right-hand lane of a three-lane motorway be used?

- ☐ **A** As a high-speed lane
- ☐ **B** As an overtaking lane
- ☐ **C** As a right-turn lane
- ☐ **D** As an acceleration lane

You should stay in the left-hand lane of a motorway unless you're overtaking another vehicle. The right-hand lane of a motorway is an overtaking lane; it isn't the 'fast lane'. After overtaking, move back to the left when it's safe to do so.

572 Mark *one* answer
Where can you find reflective amber studs on a motorway?

- ☐ **A** Separating the slip road from the motorway
- ☐ **B** On the left-hand edge of the road
- ☐ **C** On the right-hand edge of the road
- ☐ **D** Separating the lanes

At night or in poor visibility, reflective studs on the road help you to judge your position on the carriageway.

573 Mark *one* answer
Where on a motorway would you find green reflective studs?

- ☐ **A** Separating driving lanes
- ☐ **B** Between the hard shoulder and the carriageway
- ☐ **C** At slip-road entrances and exits
- ☐ **D** Between the carriageway and the central reservation

Knowing the colours of the reflective studs on the road will help you judge your position, especially at night, in foggy conditions or when visibility is poor.

574 Mark *one* answer
What should you do when you see this sign as you travel along a motorway?

☐ **A** Leave the motorway at the next exit
☐ **B** Turn left immediately
☐ **C** Change lane
☐ **D** Move onto the hard shoulder

You'll see this sign if the motorway is closed ahead. Pull into the left-hand lane as soon as it's safe to do so. Don't wait until the last moment before you move across, because the lane may be busy and you'll have to rely on another driver making room for you.

575 Mark *one* answer
What does this sign mean?

☐ **A** No motor vehicles
☐ **B** End of motorway
☐ **C** No through road
☐ **D** End of bus lane

When you leave the motorway, make sure that you check your speedometer. You may be going faster than you realise. Slow down and look for speed-limit signs.

576 Mark *one* answer
Which of these signs means that the national speed limit applies?

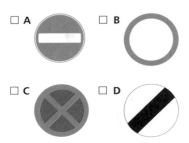

☐ **A**   ☐ **B**

☐ **C**   ☐ **D**

You should know the speed limit for the road on which you're travelling and the vehicle that you're driving. The different speed limits are shown in *The Highway Code*.

577 Mark *one* answer
What's the maximum speed on a single carriageway road?

☐ **A** 50 mph
☐ **B** 60 mph
☐ **C** 40 mph
☐ **D** 70 mph

If you're travelling on a dual carriageway that becomes a single carriageway road, reduce your speed gradually so that you aren't exceeding the limit as you enter. There might not be a sign to remind you of the limit, so make sure you know the speed limits for different types of road and vehicle.

578 Mark *one* answer
What does this sign mean?

- ☐ **A** End of motorway
- ☐ **B** End of restriction
- ☐ **C** Lane ends ahead
- ☐ **D** Free recovery ends

Temporary restrictions on motorways are shown on signs that have flashing amber lights. At the end of the restriction, you'll see this sign without any flashing lights.

---

579 Mark *one* answer
What does this sign indicate?

- ☐ **A** A diversion route
- ☐ **B** A picnic area
- ☐ **C** A pedestrian zone
- ☐ **D** A cycle route

When a diversion route has been put in place, drivers are advised to follow a symbol, which may be a black triangle, square, circle or diamond shape on a yellow background.

580 Mark *one* answer
What does this temporary sign indicate?

- ☐ **A** The speed-limit change at the end of the motorway
- ☐ **B** An advisory change of speed limit ahead
- ☐ **C** A variable speed limit ahead
- ☐ **D** A mandatory speed-limit change ahead

In the interests of road safety, temporary mandatory speed limits are imposed at all major roadworks. Signs like this, giving advance warning of the speed limit, are normally placed about three-quarters of a mile ahead of where the speed limit comes into force.

581 Mark *one* answer
What does this traffic sign mean?

- ☐ **A** Compulsory maximum speed limit
- ☐ **B** Advisory maximum speed limit
- ☐ **C** Compulsory minimum speed limit
- ☐ **D** Advised separation distance

The sign gives you an early warning of a speed restriction. If you're travelling at a higher speed, slow down in good time. You could come across queuing traffic due to roadworks or a temporary obstruction.

582 Mark *one* answer
What should you do when you see this sign at a crossroads?

- ☐ **A** Maintain the same speed
- ☐ **B** Carry on with great care
- ☐ **C** Find another route
- ☐ **D** Telephone the police

When traffic lights are out of order, treat the junction as an unmarked crossroads. Be very careful and be prepared to stop; no-one has priority.

583 Mark *one* answer
You're signalling to turn right in busy traffic. How would you confirm your intention safely?

- ☐ **A** Sound the horn
- ☐ **B** Give an arm signal
- ☐ **C** Flash your headlights
- ☐ **D** Position over the centre line

In some situations, you may feel your indicators can't be seen by other road users. If you think you need to make your intention more obvious, give the arm signal shown in *The Highway Code*.

584 Mark *one* answer
What does this sign mean?

- ☐ **A** Motorcycles only
- ☐ **B** No cars
- ☐ **C** Cars only
- ☐ **D** No motorcycles

You must comply with all traffic signs and be especially aware of those signs that apply specifically to the type of vehicle you're using.

585 Mark *one* answer

You're on a motorway. A lorry has stopped in the right-hand lane. What should you do when you see this sign on the lorry?

- ☐ **A** Move into the right-hand lane
- ☐ **B** Stop behind the flashing lights
- ☐ **C** Pass the lorry on the left
- ☐ **D** Leave the motorway at the next exit

Sometimes work is carried out on the motorway without closing the lanes. When this happens, signs are mounted on the back of lorries to warn other road users of the roadworks ahead.

586 Mark *one* answer

You're on a motorway. Red flashing lights appear above your lane only. What should you do?

- ☐ **A** Continue in that lane and look for further information
- ☐ **B** Move into another lane in good time
- ☐ **C** Pull onto the hard shoulder
- ☐ **D** Stop and wait for an instruction to proceed

Flashing red lights above your lane show that your lane is closed. You should move into another lane as soon as you can do so safely.

587 Mark *one* answer

When may you sound the horn?

- ☐ **A** To give you right of way
- ☐ **B** To attract a friend's attention
- ☐ **C** To warn others of your presence
- ☐ **D** To make slower drivers move over

Never sound the horn aggressively. You mustn't sound it when driving in a built-up area between 11.30 pm and 7.00 am, or when you're stationary, unless another road user poses a danger. Don't scare animals by sounding your horn.

588 Mark *one* answer

Your vehicle is stationary. When may you use its horn?

- ☐ **A** When another road user poses a danger
- ☐ **B** When the road is blocked by queuing traffic
- ☐ **C** When it's used only briefly
- ☐ **D** When signalling that you've just arrived

When your vehicle is stationary, only sound the horn if you think there's a risk of danger from another road user. Don't use it just to attract someone's attention. This causes unnecessary noise and could be misleading.

589 Mark *one* answer
What does this sign mean?

- ☐ **A** You can park on the days and times shown
- ☐ **B** No parking on the days and times shown
- ☐ **C** No parking at all from Monday to Friday
- ☐ **D** End of the urban clearway restrictions

Urban clearways are provided to keep traffic flowing at busy times. You may stop only briefly to set down or pick up passengers. Times of operation will vary from place to place, so always check the signs.

590 Mark *one* answer
What does this sign mean?

- ☐ **A** Quayside or river bank
- ☐ **B** Steep hill downwards
- ☐ **C** Uneven road surface
- ☐ **D** Road liable to flooding

You should be careful in these locations, as the road surface is likely to be wet and slippery. There may be a steep drop to the water, and there may not be a barrier along the edge of the road.

591 Mark *one* answer
Which sign means you have priority over oncoming vehicles?

☐ **A**  ☐ **B**

☐ **C**   ☐ **D**

Even though you have priority, be prepared to give way if other drivers don't. This will help to avoid congestion, confrontation or even a collision.

592 Mark *one* answer
What does this white line along the centre of the road mean?

- ☐ **A** Bus lane marking
- ☐ **B** Hazard warning
- ☐ **C** Give way warning
- ☐ **D** Lane marking

The centre of the road is usually marked by a broken white line, with lines that are shorter than the gaps. When the lines become longer than the gaps, this is a hazard warning line. Look well ahead for these, especially when you're planning to overtake or turn off.

593 Mark *one* answer

What's the reason for the yellow crisscross lines painted on the road here?

- ☐ **A** To mark out an area for trams only
- ☐ **B** To prevent queuing traffic from blocking the junction on the left
- ☐ **C** To mark the entrance lane to a car park
- ☐ **D** To warn you of the tram lines crossing the road

Yellow 'box junctions' like this are often used where it's busy. Their purpose is to keep the junction clear for crossing traffic. Don't enter the painted area unless your exit is clear. The one exception is when you're turning right and are only prevented from doing so by oncoming traffic or by other vehicles waiting to turn right.

594 Mark *one* answer

What's the reason for the hatched area along the centre of this road?

- ☐ **A** It separates traffic flowing in opposite directions
- ☐ **B** It marks an area to be used by overtaking motorcyclists
- ☐ **C** It's a temporary marking to warn of the roadworks
- ☐ **D** It separates the two sides of the dual carriageway

Areas of 'hatched markings' such as these separate traffic streams that could be a danger to each other. They're often seen on bends or where the road becomes narrow. If the area is bordered by a solid white line, you mustn't enter it except in an emergency.

595 Mark *one* answer

Other drivers may sometimes flash their headlights at you. In which situation are they allowed to do this?

- ☐ **A** To warn of a radar speed trap ahead
- ☐ **B** To show that they're giving way to you
- ☐ **C** To warn you of their presence
- ☐ **D** To let you know there's a fault with your vehicle

If other drivers flash their headlights, this isn't a signal to show priority. The flashing of headlights has the same meaning as sounding the horn: it's a warning of their presence.

596 Mark *one* answer
What speed limit is often found in narrow residential streets?

☐ **A** 20 mph
☐ **B** 25 mph
☐ **C** 35 mph
☐ **D** 40 mph

In some built-up areas, you may find the speed limit reduced to 20 mph. Driving at a slower speed will help give you the time and space to see and deal safely with hazards such as pedestrians and other vulnerable road users.

597 Mark *one* answer
What does this signal mean?

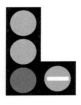

☐ **A** Cars must stop
☐ **B** Trams must stop
☐ **C** Both trams and cars must stop
☐ **D** Both trams and cars can continue

The white light shows that trams must stop. The green light shows that other vehicles can go if the way is clear. Trams are being introduced into more cities, so you're likely to come across them and you should learn which signs apply to them.

598 Mark *one* answer
Where would you find these road markings?

☐ **A** At a railway crossing
☐ **B** At a mini-roundabout
☐ **C** On a motorway
☐ **D** On a pedestrian crossing

These markings show the direction in which the traffic should go at a mini-roundabout.

599 Mark *one* answer
A police car is following you. The police officer flashes the headlights and points to the left. What should you do?

☐ **A** Turn left at the next junction
☐ **B** Pull up on the left
☐ **C** Stop immediately
☐ **D** Move over to the left

You must pull up on the left as soon as it's safe to do so and switch off your engine.

600 Mark *one* answer

You see this amber traffic light ahead. Which light, or lights, will come on next?

- ☐ **A** Red alone
- ☐ **B** Red and amber together
- ☐ **C** Green and amber together
- ☐ **D** Green alone

At junctions controlled by traffic lights, you must stop behind the white line until the lights change to green. A red light, an amber light, and red and amber lights showing together all mean stop.

You may proceed when the light is green unless your exit road is blocked or pedestrians are crossing in front of you.

If you're approaching traffic lights that are visible from a distance and the light has been green for some time, be ready to slow down and stop, because the lights are likely to change.

601 Mark *one* answer

You see this signal overhead on the motorway. What does it mean?

- ☐ **A** Leave the motorway at the next exit
- ☐ **B** All vehicles use the hard shoulder
- ☐ **C** Sharp bend to the left ahead
- ☐ **D** Stop: all lanes ahead closed

You'll see this sign if there has been an incident ahead and the motorway is closed. You must obey the sign. Make sure that you prepare to leave in good time.

Don't cause drivers to take avoiding action by cutting in at the last moment.

602 Mark *one* answer

What MUST you do when you see this sign?

- ☐ **A** Stop only if traffic is approaching
- ☐ **B** Stop even if the road is clear
- ☐ **C** Stop only if children are waiting to cross
- ☐ **D** Stop only if a red light is showing

'Stop' signs are situated at junctions where visibility is restricted or where there's heavy traffic. They must be obeyed: you must stop.

Take good all-round observation before moving off.

603 Mark *one* answer
Which shape is used for a 'give way' sign?

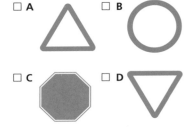

☐ A   ☐ B   ☐ C   ☐ D

Other warning signs are the same shape and colour, but the 'give way' triangle points downwards. When you see this sign, you must give way to traffic on the road that you're about to enter.

604 Mark *one* answer
What does this sign mean?

☐ **A** Buses turning
☐ **B** Ring road
☐ **C** Mini-roundabout
☐ **D** Keep right

When you see this sign, look out for any direction signs and judge whether you need to signal your intentions. Do this in good time so that other road users approaching the roundabout know what you're planning to do.

605 Mark *one* answer
What does this sign mean?

☐ **A** Two-way traffic straight ahead
☐ **B** Two-way traffic crosses a one-way road
☐ **C** Two-way traffic over a bridge
☐ **D** Two-way traffic crosses a two-way road

Be prepared for traffic approaching from junctions on either side of you. Try to avoid unnecessary changing of lanes just before the junction.

606 Mark *one* answer
What does this sign mean?

☐ **A** Two-way traffic crosses a one-way road
☐ **B** Traffic approaching you has priority
☐ **C** Two-way traffic straight ahead
☐ **D** Motorway contraflow system ahead

This sign may be at the end of a dual carriageway or a one-way street. It's there to warn you of oncoming traffic.

607 Mark *one* answer
What does this sign mean?

- ☐ **A** Hump bridge
- ☐ **B** Traffic-calming hump
- ☐ **C** Low bridge
- ☐ **D** Uneven road

You'll need to slow down. At hump bridges, your view ahead will be restricted and the road will often be narrow. If the bridge is very steep, sound your horn to warn others of your approach. Going over the bridge too fast is highly dangerous to other road users and could even cause your wheels to leave the road, with a resulting loss of control.

608 Mark *one* answer
Which sign informs you that you're coming to a 'no through road'?

This sign is found at the entrance to a road that can only be used for access.

609 Mark *one* answer
What does this sign mean?

- ☐ **A** Direction to park-and-ride car park
- ☐ **B** No parking for buses or coaches
- ☐ **C** Direction to bus and coach park
- ☐ **D** Parking area for cars and coaches

To ease the congestion in town centres, some cities and towns provide park-and-ride schemes. These allow you to park in a designated area and ride by bus into the centre.

Park-and-ride schemes are usually cheaper and easier than car parking in the town centre.

610   Mark *one* answer

What should you do when approaching traffic lights where red and amber are showing together?

☐ **A** Pass the lights if the road is clear
☐ **B** Take care because there's a fault with the lights
☐ **C** Wait for the green light
☐ **D** Stop because the lights are changing to red

Be aware that other traffic might still be clearing the junction as you approach. A green light means you may go on, but only if the way is clear.

611   Mark *one* answer

Where does this marking normally appear on a road?

☐ **A** Just before a 'no entry' sign
☐ **B** Just before a 'give way' sign
☐ **C** Just before a 'stop' sign
☐ **D** Just before a 'no through road' sign

This road marking means you should give way to traffic on the main road. It might not be used at junctions where there isn't much traffic. However, if there's a double broken line across the junction, the 'give way' rules still apply.

612   Mark *one* answer

At a railway level crossing, the red lights continue to flash after a train has gone by. What should you do?

☐ **A** Phone the signal operator
☐ **B** Alert drivers behind you
☐ **C** Wait
☐ **D** Proceed with caution

You must always obey red flashing stop lights. If a train passes but the lights continue to flash, another train will be passing soon. Cross only when the lights go off and the barriers open.

613   Mark *one* answer

You're in a tunnel and you see this sign. What does it mean?

☐ **A** Direction to emergency pedestrian exit
☐ **B** Beware of pedestrians: no footpath ahead
☐ **C** No access for pedestrians
☐ **D** Beware of pedestrians crossing ahead

If you have to leave your vehicle and get out of a tunnel by an emergency exit, do so as quickly as you can. Follow the signs directing you to the nearest exit point. If there are several people using the exit, don't panic but try to leave in a calm and orderly manner.

614 Mark *one* answer

Which of these signs shows that you're entering a one-way system?

☐ A   ☐ B   ☐ C   ☐ D

If the road has two lanes, you can use either lane and overtake on either side. Use the lane that's more convenient for your destination unless signs or road markings indicate otherwise.

615 Mark *one* answer

What does this sign mean?

☐ **A** With-flow bus and cycle lane
☐ **B** Contraflow bus and cycle lane
☐ **C** No buses and cycles allowed
☐ **D** No waiting for buses and cycles

Buses and cycles can travel in this lane. In this example, they'll flow in the same direction as other traffic. If it's busy, they may be passing you on the left, so watch out for them. Times on the sign will show the lane's hours of operation; if no times are shown, or there's no sign at all, this means the lane is in operation 24 hours a day. In some areas, other vehicles, such as taxis and motorcycles, are allowed to use bus lanes. The sign will show if this is the case.

616 Mark *one* answer
Which of these signs warns you of a zebra crossing?

☐ A   ☐ B

☐ C   ☐ D

Look well ahead and check the pavements and surrounding areas for pedestrians. Look for anyone walking towards the crossing. Check your mirrors for traffic behind, in case you have to slow down or stop.

617 Mark *one* answer
What does this sign mean?

☐ **A** School crossing patrol
☐ **B** No pedestrians allowed
☐ **C** Pedestrian zone – no vehicles
☐ **D** Zebra crossing ahead

Look well ahead and be ready to stop for any pedestrians crossing, or about to cross, the road. Also check the pavements for anyone who looks like they might step or run into the road.

618 Mark *one* answer
Which sign means there will be two-way traffic crossing your route ahead?

☐ A   ☐ B

☐ C   ☐ D

This sign is found in or at the end of a one-way system. It warns you that traffic will be crossing your path from both directions.

619 Mark *one* answer
Which arm signal tells you that the car you're following is going to pull up?

☐ A   ☐ B

☐ C   ☐ D

There may be occasions when drivers need to give an arm signal to confirm their intentions. This could include in bright sunshine, at a complex road layout, when stopping at a pedestrian crossing or when turning right just after passing a parked vehicle. You should understand what each arm signal means. If you give arm signals, make them clear, correct and decisive.

620 Mark *one* answer

Which of these signs means turn left ahead?

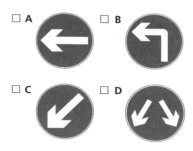

☐ A   ☐ B

☐ C   ☐ D

Blue circles tell you what you must do and this sign gives a clear instruction to turn left ahead. You should be looking out for signs at all times and know what they mean.

621 Mark *one* answer

What should you be aware of if you've just passed this sign?

☐ **A** This is a single-track road
☐ **B** You can't stop on this road
☐ **C** Only one lane is in use
☐ **D** All traffic is going one way

In a one-way system, traffic may pass you on either side. Always be aware of all traffic signs and understand their meaning. Look well ahead and react to them in good time.

622 Mark *one* answer

You're approaching a red traffic light. What will the signal show next?

☐ **A** Red and amber
☐ **B** Green alone
☐ **C** Amber alone
☐ **D** Green and amber

If you know which light is going to show next, you can plan your approach accordingly. This can help prevent excessive braking or hesitation at the junction.

623 Mark *one* answer

What does this sign mean?

☐ **A** Low bridge ahead
☐ **B** Tunnel ahead
☐ **C** Ancient monument ahead
☐ **D** Traffic danger spot ahead

When approaching a tunnel, switch on your dipped headlights. Be aware that your eyes might need to adjust to the sudden darkness. You may need to reduce your speed.

624 Mark *one* answer
What information is found on a vehicle registration document?

☐ **A** The make and model
☐ **B** The service history
☐ **C** The ignition-key security number
☐ **D** The original purchase price

Every vehicle should have a registration document showing the registered keeper. It's your legal responsibility to make sure all the information is correct. This includes make, model and engine size. If you buy a new vehicle, the dealer will register it with DVLA, who will send the registration document to you.

625 Mark *one* answer ▮NI▮
Who can carry out compulsory basic training (CBT)?

☐ **A** Any approved driving instructor (ADI)
☐ **B** Any road safety officer
☐ **C** Any Driver and Vehicle Standards Agency (DVSA)-approved training body
☐ **D** Any motorcycle main dealer

CBT courses can only be given by training bodies that are approved by DVSA. The standard of training is monitored by DVSA examiners. The course is designed to give you basic skills before riding on the road.

626 Mark *one* answer
What should you be sure of before riding anyone else's motorcycle?

☐ **A** That the owner has third-party insurance cover
☐ **B** That your own motorcycle has insurance cover
☐ **C** That the motorcycle is insured for your use
☐ **D** That the owner has the insurance documents with them

If you borrow a motorcycle, you must make sure that you're insured to ride it. It's better to find this out for yourself, rather than taking somebody else's word for it.

627 Mark *one* answer ▮NI▮
How long after first registration must a motorcycle have its first MOT test?

☐ **A** One year
☐ **B** Three years
☐ **C** Five years
☐ **D** Seven years

Any motorcycle you ride must be in good condition and roadworthy. If it's over three years old, it must have a valid MOT test certificate (unless it's exempt from the MOT test – see GOV.UK).

628 Mark *one* answer
What information can be found on a motorcycle's registration document?

☐ **A** The registered keeper's name
☐ **B** The type of insurance cover required
☐ **C** The service history
☐ **D** The date of the MOT

Every vehicle on the road has a registration document. This records any change of ownership and gives specific information relating to the vehicle and owner. This includes the date of first registration, the registration number, the make and colour of the vehicle, and the registered keeper's name.

629 Mark *one* answer
You own a motorcycle licensed in the UK. When do you have a duty to contact the Driver and Vehicle Licensing Agency (DVLA)?

☐ **A** When you go abroad on holiday
☐ **B** When your job involves riding abroad
☐ **C** When your permanent address changes
☐ **D** When you change your job status

DVLA need to keep their records up to date. They'll send you a reminder when you need to tax your vehicle. To do this, they need your current address. Every vehicle in the country is registered so that its history can be traced.

630 Mark *one* answer
Your motorcycle is insured third-party only. What does this cover?

☐ **A** Damage to your motorcycle
☐ **B** All damage and injury
☐ **C** Injury to yourself
☐ **D** Injury to others

Third-party insurance is usually cheaper than comprehensive insurance. It covers injuries to other people and damage to their property, but it doesn't cover any damage to your own motorcycle or property. Nor does it provide cover if your motorcycle is stolen.

631 Mark *one* answer
What's the legal minimum insurance cover you must have to ride on public roads?

☐ **A** Third-party, fire and theft
☐ **B** Comprehensive
☐ **C** Third-party only
☐ **D** Personal injury cover

The minimum insurance cover required by law is third-party only. This covers the other people and vehicles involved in a collision, but not you or your vehicle. Also, basic third-party insurance won't cover you for theft or fire damage. Make sure you read your policy carefully and understand what it covers.

632 Mark *one* answer
What does a motorcycle registration document show?

☐ **A** The service history
☐ **B** The year of first registration
☐ **C** The purchase price
☐ **D** The tyre sizes

A motorcycle registration document contains a number of details that are unique to a particular vehicle. You must notify the DVLA of any changes to, for example, the registered keeper or registration number. You must also tell them about any modifications made to the motorcycle.

633 Mark *one* answer
What's the purpose of an MOT test?

☐ **A** To make sure your motorcycle is roadworthy
☐ **B** To certify how many miles per gallon it does
☐ **C** To prove you own the motorcycle
☐ **D** To allow you to park in restricted areas

It's your responsibility to make sure that any motorcycle you ride is in a roadworthy condition. Any faults that develop should be corrected promptly. If your motorcycle fails an MOT test, it shouldn't be used on the road unless you're taking it to have the faults repaired or for a previously arranged retest.

634 Mark *one* answer   NI
What do you need before you can take a practical motorcycle test?

☐ **A** A valid full moped licence
☐ **B** A valid full car licence
☐ **C** A valid compulsory basic training (CBT) certificate
☐ **D** 12 months' riding experience

The purpose of a CBT course is to teach you basic theory and practical skills before you ride on the road, on your own, for the first time. CBT courses can only be given by approved training bodies (ATBs).

635 Mark *one* answer
When must you notify the licensing authority?

☐ **A** When your insurance is due for renewal
☐ **B** When you have a medical condition that affects your riding
☐ **C** When you intend to take your motorcycle abroad on holiday
☐ **D** When you wish to renew your motorcycle's MOT certificate

The licensing authorities hold the records of all vehicles, drivers and riders in Great Britain and Northern Ireland. They need to keep their records up to date and you must notify them if any aspect of your health affects your ability to ride your motorcycle.

636 Mark *one* answer
You've just passed your practical motorcycle test. This is your first full licence. What will you have to do if you gather six or more penalty points within the next two years?

☐ **A** Retake only your theory test
☐ **B** Reapply for your full licence immediately
☐ **C** Retake only your practical test
☐ **D** Reapply for your provisional licence

If the number of points on your licence reaches six or more during your first two years of holding a full licence, your licence will be revoked. This includes offences you committed before you passed your test. You may ride only as a learner until you pass both the theory and practical tests again.

637 Mark *one* answer
You hold a provisional motorcycle licence. What does this licence restrict you from doing?

☐ **A** Exceeding 30 mph
☐ **B** Riding on a dual carriageway
☐ **C** Riding after dark
☐ **D** Carrying a pillion passenger

Provisional entitlement means that restrictions apply to your use of motorcycles. For example, you may not ride on a motorway or carry a passenger. The requirements are there to protect you and other road users. Make sure you're aware of all the restrictions that apply before you ride your motorcycle on the road.

638 Mark *one* answer
What's the maximum engine size a full category A1 motorcycle licence will allow you to ride?

☐ **A** 125 cc
☐ **B** 250 cc
☐ **C** 350 cc
☐ **D** 425 cc

When you pass your test on a motorcycle between 120 cc and 125 cc, you'll be issued with a full light motorcycle licence of category A1. You'll then be allowed to ride any motorcycle up to 125 cc and with a power output not exceeding 11 kW (14.6 bhp).

639 Mark *one* answer   NI
Do you need to display L plates when learning to ride a motorcycle under the direct access scheme?

☐ **A** No, you don't need L plates if you've passed a car test
☐ **B** Yes, you need L plates only when learning on your own machine
☐ **C** Yes, you need L plates while learning with a qualified instructor
☐ **D** No, you don't need L plates if you've passed a moped test

When training under the direct access scheme, you must be accompanied by an instructor on another motorcycle, who must be in radio contact with you. You must display red L plates to the front and rear of your motorcycle and follow all normal learner restrictions.

640 Mark *one* answer NI

A motorcyclist is riding a motorcycle that has an engine larger than 50 cc. When may they carry a pillion passenger?

☐ **A** When the rider has successfully completed CBT (compulsory basic training)
☐ **B** When the rider holds a full licence for the category of motorcycle they're riding
☐ **C** When no sidecar is fitted to the machine
☐ **D** When the rider has a full car licence and is over 21

Before carrying a passenger on a motorcycle, the rider must hold a full licence for the category of motorcycle being ridden. They must also ensure that a proper passenger seat and footrests are fitted.

641 Mark *one* answer NI

You have a CBT (compulsory basic training) certificate. How long is it valid?

☐ **A** One year
☐ **B** Two years
☐ **C** Three years
☐ **D** Four years

All new learner motorcycle and moped riders must complete a CBT course before riding on the road. This can only be given by an approved training body (ATB). If you don't pass your practical test within two years, you'll need to retake and pass CBT to continue riding.

642 Mark *one* answer

Your vehicle tax is due to expire. To renew it, you'll need a renewal form, the fee and a valid MOT (if applicable). What else will you need?

☐ **A** Proof of purchase
☐ **B** A CBT certificate
☐ **C** A valid certificate of insurance
☐ **D** A complete service record

You'll normally be sent a reminder automatically by the DVLA close to the time of renewal. Make sure that all your documentation is correct, up to date and valid. You can renew online, by phone or at certain post offices.

643 Mark *one* answer

What must you have to legally carry a pillion passenger on your motorcycle?

☐ **A** A motorcycle with an engine larger than 125 cc
☐ **B** A passenger who holds a full motorcycle licence
☐ **C** A full motorcycle licence
☐ **D** Three years' motorcycle riding experience

As a learner motorcyclist, you aren't allowed to carry a pillion passenger, even if they hold a full motorcycle licence. You mustn't carry a passenger, or tow a trailer, until you've passed your test.

644 Mark *one* answer

A friend asks you to give them a lift on your motorcycle. What conditions apply?

- ☐ **A** Your motorcycle must be larger than 125 cc
- ☐ **B** You must have three years' motorcycle riding experience
- ☐ **C** The pillion passenger must hold a full motorcycle licence
- ☐ **D** You must have a full motorcycle licence

By law, you can only carry a pillion passenger after you've gained a full motorcycle licence. It makes no difference if the passenger holds a full licence. As a learner, you're also prohibited from towing a trailer or riding on motorways.

645 Mark *one* answer

Your motorcycle insurance policy has an excess of £100. What does this mean?

- ☐ **A** The insurance company will pay the first £100 of any claim
- ☐ **B** You'll be paid £100 if you don't have a crash
- ☐ **C** Your motorcycle is insured for a value of £100 if it's stolen
- ☐ **D** You'll have to pay the first £100 of any claim

This is a method used by insurance companies to keep annual premiums down. Generally, the higher the excess you choose to pay, the lower the annual premium you'll be charged.

646 Mark *one* answer

For how long is an MOT certificate normally valid?

- ☐ **A** Three years after the date it was issued
- ☐ **B** 10,000 miles
- ☐ **C** One year after the date it was issued
- ☐ **D** 30,000 miles

Some garages will remind you that your vehicle is due for its annual MOT test, but not all do. To ensure continuous cover, you may take your vehicle for its MOT up to one month before its existing MOT certificate runs out. The expiry date on the new certificate will be 12 months after the expiry date on the old certificate.

647 Mark *one* answer

What is a cover note?

- ☐ **A** A document issued before you receive your driving licence
- ☐ **B** A document issued before you receive your insurance certificate
- ☐ **C** A document issued before you receive your registration document
- ☐ **D** A document issued before you receive your MOT certificate

Sometimes an insurance company will issue a temporary insurance certificate called a cover note. It gives you the same insurance cover as your certificate but lasts for a limited period, usually one month.

648 Mark *one* answer

You've just passed your practical test. You don't hold a full licence in another category. Within two years you get six penalty points on your licence. What will you have to do?

☐ **A** Retake only your theory test
☐ **B** Retake your theory and practical tests
☐ **C** Retake only your practical test
☐ **D** Reapply for your full licence immediately

If you accumulate six or more penalty points within two years of gaining your first full licence, it will be revoked. The six or more points include any gained due to offences you committed before passing your test. If this happens, you may only drive as a learner until you pass both the theory and practical tests again.

649 Mark *one* answer

For how long is a Statutory Off-Road Notification (SORN) valid?

☐ **A** Until the vehicle is taxed, sold or scrapped
☐ **B** Until the vehicle is insured and MOT'd
☐ **C** Until the vehicle is repaired or modified
☐ **D** Until the vehicle is used on the road

A SORN allows you to keep a vehicle off-road and untaxed. SORN will end when the vehicle is taxed, sold or scrapped.

650 Mark *one* answer

What is a Statutory Off-Road Notification (SORN)?

☐ **A** A notification to tell the DVSA that a vehicle doesn't have a current MOT
☐ **B** Information kept by the police about the owner of a vehicle
☐ **C** A notification to tell the DVLA that a vehicle isn't being used on the road
☐ **D** Information held by insurance companies to check a vehicle is insured

If you want to keep a vehicle untaxed and off the public road, you must make a SORN. It's an offence not to do so. Your SORN is valid until your vehicle is taxed, sold or scrapped.

651 Mark *one* answer **NI**

What's the maximum fine for driving without insurance?

☐ **A** Unlimited
☐ **B** £500
☐ **C** £1000
☐ **D** £5000

Driving without insurance is a serious offence. As well as an unlimited fine, you may be disqualified or incur penalty points.

652 Mark *one* answer

Who's legally responsible for ensuring that a vehicle registration certificate (V5C) is updated?

- ☐ **A** The registered vehicle keeper
- ☐ **B** The vehicle manufacturer
- ☐ **C** Your insurance company
- ☐ **D** The licensing authority

It's your legal responsibility to keep the details on your vehicle registration certificate (V5C) up to date. You should tell the licensing authority about any changes. These include your name, address or vehicle details. If you don't do this, you may have problems when you try to sell your vehicle.

653 Mark *one* answer

In which of these circumstances must you show your insurance certificate?

- ☐ **A** When making a SORN
- ☐ **B** When buying or selling a vehicle
- ☐ **C** When a police officer asks you for it
- ☐ **D** When having an MOT inspection

You must produce a valid insurance certificate when requested by a police officer. If you can't do this immediately, you may be asked to take it to a police station. Other documents you may be asked to produce are your driving licence and the vehicle's MOT certificate.

654 Mark *one* answer

Your vehicle must have valid insurance cover before you can do what?

- ☐ **A** Make a SORN
- ☐ **B** Sell the vehicle
- ☐ **C** Scrap the vehicle
- ☐ **D** Tax the vehicle

Your vehicle must have valid insurance cover before you can tax it. If required, it will also need to have a valid MOT certificate. You can tax your vehicle online, by phone or at certain post offices.

655 Mark *one* answer

Your vehicle needs a current MOT certificate. What will the MOT certificate enable you to do?

- ☐ **A** Renew your driving licence
- ☐ **B** Change your insurance company
- ☐ **C** Tax your vehicle
- ☐ **D** Notify a change of address

If your vehicle is required to have an MOT certificate, you'll need to make sure this is current before you're able to tax your vehicle. You can do this online, by phone or at certain post offices.

656 Mark *one* answer

Which of these is needed before you can legally use a vehicle on the road?

☐ **A** A valid driving licence
☐ **B** Breakdown cover
☐ **C** Proof of your identity
☐ **D** A vehicle handbook

Using a vehicle on the road illegally carries a heavy fine and can lead to penalty points on your driving licence. You must have
• a valid driving licence
• paid the appropriate vehicle tax
• proper insurance cover.

657 Mark *one* answer

What must you have when you apply to renew your vehicle tax?

☐ **A** Valid insurance
☐ **B** The vehicle's chassis number
☐ **C** The handbook
☐ **D** A valid driving licence

You can renew your vehicle tax online, at post offices and vehicle registration offices, or by phone. When applying, make sure you have all the relevant valid documents, including a valid MOT test certificate where applicable.

658 Mark *one* answer

A police officer asks to see your documents. You don't have them with you. Within what time must you produce them at a police station?

☐ **A** 5 days
☐ **B** 7 days
☐ **C** 14 days
☐ **D** 21 days

You don't have to carry around your vehicle's documents wherever you go. If a police officer asks to see them and you don't have them with you, you may be asked to produce them at a police station within 7 days.

659 Mark *one* answer

When should you update your vehicle registration certificate?

☐ **A** When you pass your driving test
☐ **B** When you move house
☐ **C** When your vehicle needs an MOT
☐ **D** When you have a collision

As the registered keeper of a vehicle, it's up to you to inform the DVLA of any changes in your details; for example, your name or address. You do this by completing and sending off the relevant section of the registration certificate.

660 Mark *one* answer

Your motorcycle has broken down on a motorway. How will you know the direction of the nearest emergency telephone?

- ☐ **A** By walking with the flow of traffic
- ☐ **B** By following an arrow on a marker post
- ☐ **C** By walking against the flow of traffic
- ☐ **D** By remembering where the last phone was

If you break down on a motorway, pull onto the hard shoulder and stop as far over to the left as you can. Switch on your hazard warning lights (if fitted) and go to the nearest emergency telephone. Marker posts spaced every 100 metres will show you where the nearest telephone is.

661 Mark *one* answer

When should you use the engine cut-out switch?

- ☐ **A** To stop the engine in an emergency
- ☐ **B** To stop the engine after a short journey
- ☐ **C** To save wear on the ignition switch
- ☐ **D** To start the engine if you lose the key

Most motorcycles are fitted with an engine cut-out switch. This is designed to stop the engine in an emergency and so reduce the risk of electrical sparks starting a fire.

662 Mark *one* answer

You're riding on a motorway. The car in front switches on its hazard warning lights while it's moving. What does this mean?

- ☐ **A** The driver is going to take the next exit
- ☐ **B** There's danger ahead
- ☐ **C** There's a police car ahead
- ☐ **D** The driver is trying to change lanes

Drivers and riders may switch on their hazard warning lights to warn following traffic of an obstruction or danger ahead. This only applies on motorways and dual carriageways that are subject to the national speed limit. The hazard warning lights should be turned off again when it's clear the warning has been seen.

663 Mark *one* answer

What will you be asked when you use the emergency telephone on a motorway?

- ☐ **A** The number of the telephone you're using
- ☐ **B** The number on your driving licence
- ☐ **C** The name of your vehicle insurance company
- ☐ **D** The route you were taking before the breakdown

Have information about your motorcycle and the number of the phone you're using ready before you call from an emergency telephone. For your own safety, face the traffic during the call.

664 Mark *one* answer

You're on a motorway. When can you use hazard warning lights?

- ☐ **A** When a vehicle is following too closely
- ☐ **B** When you slow down quickly because of danger ahead
- ☐ **C** When you're being towed by another vehicle
- ☐ **D** When you're riding on the hard shoulder

Briefly using your hazard warning lights will warn the traffic behind you that there's a hazard ahead. Turn them off again when following drivers have seen and responded to your signal.

665 Mark *one* answer

You're riding through a tunnel. What should you do if your motorcycle breaks down?

- ☐ **A** Switch on hazard warning lights
- ☐ **B** Remain on your motorcycle
- ☐ **C** Wait for the police to find you
- ☐ **D** Rely on CCTV cameras seeing you

If your motorcycle breaks down in a tunnel, it could present a danger to other traffic. First switch on your hazard warning lights and then call for help from an emergency telephone point. Don't rely on being found by the police or being seen by a CCTV camera.

666 Mark *one* answer

You're on a motorway. Luggage falls from your motorcycle. What should you do?

- ☐ **A** Stop at the next emergency telephone and report the hazard
- ☐ **B** Stop on the motorway and put on hazard warning lights while you pick it up
- ☐ **C** Walk back up the motorway to pick it up
- ☐ **D** Pull up on the hard shoulder and wave traffic down

If any of your luggage falls onto the road, pull onto the hard shoulder near an emergency telephone and call for assistance. Don't stop on the carriageway or attempt to retrieve anything.

667 Mark *one* answer

You're involved in a collision with another vehicle. Someone is injured and your motorcycle is damaged. What should you find out?

- ☐ **A** Whether the driver owns the other vehicle involved
- ☐ **B** Whether the other driver is licensed to drive
- ☐ **C** The occupation of the other driver
- ☐ **D** The other driver's vehicle insurance details

If you're involved in a collision where someone is injured, your first priority is to warn other traffic and call the emergency services. Make sure you have all the information you need before you leave the scene – such as the other driver's name, phone number and insurance details. Don't ride your motorcycle if it's unroadworthy.

668 Mark *one* answer
You see a car on the hard shoulder of a motorway with a 'help' pennant displayed. What does this mean?

- ☐ **A** The driver is likely to be a disabled person
- ☐ **B** The driver is first-aid trained
- ☐ **C** The driver is a foreign visitor
- ☐ **D** The driver is a rescue patrol officer

If a disabled driver's vehicle breaks down and they're unable to walk to an emergency phone, they're advised to stay in their car and switch on the hazard warning lights. They may also display a 'help' pennant in their vehicle.

669 Mark *one* answer
When are you allowed to use hazard warning lights?

- ☐ **A** When stopped and temporarily obstructing traffic
- ☐ **B** When travelling during darkness without headlights
- ☐ **C** When parked on double yellow lines to visit a shop
- ☐ **D** When travelling slowly because you're lost

You mustn't use hazard warning lights while moving, except to warn traffic behind when you slow suddenly on a motorway or unrestricted dual carriageway.
  Never use hazard warning lights to excuse dangerous or illegal parking.

670 Mark *one* answer
You're going through a congested tunnel and have to stop. What should you do?

- ☐ **A** Pull up very close to the vehicle in front to save space
- ☐ **B** Ignore any message signs, as they're never up-to-date
- ☐ **C** Keep a safe distance from the vehicle in front
- ☐ **D** Make a U-turn and find another route

It's important to keep a safe distance from the vehicle in front at all times. This still applies in congested tunnels, even if you're moving very slowly or have stopped. If the vehicle in front breaks down, you may need room to manoeuvre past it.

671 Mark *one* answer
On a motorway, when should the hard shoulder be used?

- ☐ **A** When answering a mobile phone
- ☐ **B** When an emergency arises
- ☐ **C** When taking a short rest
- ☐ **D** When checking a road map

The hard shoulder should only be used in a genuine emergency. If possible, and if it's safe, use a roadside telephone to call for help. This will give your exact location to the operator. Never cross the carriageway or a slip road to use a telephone on the other side of the road.

672 Mark *one* answer

You arrive at the scene of a crash where someone is bleeding heavily from a wound in their arm. Nothing is embedded in the wound. What could you do to help?

☐ **A** Walk them around and keep them talking
☐ **B** Dab the wound
☐ **C** Get them a drink
☐ **D** Apply pressure over the wound

If possible, lay the casualty down. Protect yourself from exposure to blood and, when you're sure there's nothing in the wound, apply firm pressure to it using clean material.

673 Mark *one* answer

You're at an incident. What could you do to help a casualty who's unconscious?

☐ **A** Take photographs of the scene
☐ **B** Check that they're breathing normally
☐ **C** Move them to somewhere more comfortable
☐ **D** Splash their face with cool water

If a casualty is unconscious, you need to check that they're breathing normally. Look for chest movements, look and listen for breathing, and feel for breath on your cheek.

674 Mark *one* answer

Following a collision, someone has suffered a burn. The burn needs to be cooled. What's the shortest time it should be cooled for?

☐ **A** 5 minutes
☐ **B** 10 minutes
☐ **C** 15 minutes
☐ **D** 20 minutes

Check the casualty for shock and, if possible, try to cool the burn for at least 10 minutes using clean, cool water.

675 Mark *one* answer

A casualty isn't breathing normally and needs CPR. At what rate should you press down and release on the centre of their chest?

☐ **A** 10 times per minute
☐ **B** 120 times per minute
☐ **C** 60 times per minute
☐ **D** 240 times per minute

If a casualty isn't breathing normally, cardiopulmonary resuscitation (CPR) may be needed to maintain circulation. Place two hands on the centre of the chest and press down hard and fast – around 5–6 centimetres and about twice a second.

676 Mark *one* answer

A person has been injured. They may be suffering from shock. What are the warning signs to look for?

- ☐ **A** Flushed complexion
- ☐ **B** Warm dry skin
- ☐ **C** Slow pulse
- ☐ **D** Pale grey skin

The effects of shock may not be immediately obvious. Warning signs are rapid pulse, sweating, pale grey skin and rapid shallow breathing.

677 Mark *one* answer

An injured person has been placed in the recovery position. They're unconscious but breathing normally. What else should be done?

- ☐ **A** Press firmly between their shoulders
- ☐ **B** Place their arms by their side
- ☐ **C** Give them a hot sweet drink
- ☐ **D** Check their airway remains open

After a casualty has been placed in the recovery position, make sure their airway remains open and monitor their condition until medical help arrives. Where possible, don't move a casualty unless there's further danger.

678 Mark *one* answer

An injured motorcyclist is lying unconscious in the road. The traffic has stopped and there's no further danger. What should you do to help?

- ☐ **A** Remove their safety helmet
- ☐ **B** Seek medical assistance
- ☐ **C** Move the person off the road
- ☐ **D** Remove their leather jacket

If someone has been injured, the sooner proper medical attention is given the better. Ask someone to phone for help or do it yourself. An injured person should only be moved if they're in further danger. An injured motorcyclist's helmet shouldn't be removed unless it's essential.

679 Mark *one* answer

What should you do if you see a large box fall from a lorry onto the motorway?

- ☐ **A** Go to the next emergency telephone and report the hazard
- ☐ **B** Catch up with the lorry and try to get the driver's attention
- ☐ **C** Stop close to the box until the police arrive
- ☐ **D** Pull over to the hard shoulder, then remove the box

Lorry drivers can be unaware of objects falling from their vehicles. If you see something fall onto a motorway, look to see if the driver pulls over. If they don't stop, don't attempt to retrieve the object yourself. Pull onto the hard shoulder near an emergency telephone and report the hazard.

680 Mark *one* answer
You're going through a long tunnel. What will warn you of congestion or an incident ahead?

- ☐ **A** Hazard warning lines
- ☐ **B** Other drivers flashing their lights
- ☐ **C** Variable message signs
- ☐ **D** Areas with hatch markings

Follow the instructions given by the signs or by tunnel officials. In congested tunnels, a minor incident can soon turn into a major one, with serious or even fatal results.

681 Mark *one* answer
An adult casualty isn't breathing. To maintain circulation, CPR should be given. What's the correct depth to press down on their chest?

- ☐ **A** 1 to 2 centimetres
- ☐ **B** 5 to 6 centimetres
- ☐ **C** 10 to 15 centimetres
- ☐ **D** 15 to 20 centimetres

An adult casualty isn't breathing normally. To maintain circulation, place two hands on the centre of the chest. Then press down hard and fast – around 5–6 centimetres and about twice a second.

682 Mark *one* answer
You're the first to arrive at the scene of a crash. What should you do?

- ☐ **A** Leave as soon as another motorist arrives
- ☐ **B** Flag down other motorists to help you
- ☐ **C** Drag all casualties away from the vehicles
- ☐ **D** Call the emergency services promptly

At a crash scene you can help in practical ways, even if you aren't trained in first aid. Call the emergency services and make sure you don't put yourself or anyone else in danger. The safest way to warn other traffic is by switching on your hazard warning lights.

683 Mark *one* answer
You're the first person to arrive at an incident where people are badly injured. You've switched on your hazard warning lights and checked all engines are stopped. What else should you do?

- ☐ **A** Make sure that an ambulance is called for
- ☐ **B** Stop other cars and ask the drivers for help
- ☐ **C** Try and get people who are injured to drink something
- ☐ **D** Move the people who are injured clear of their vehicles

If you're the first to arrive at a crash scene, the first concerns are the risk of further collision and fire. Ensuring that vehicle engines are switched off will reduce the risk of fire. Use hazard warning lights so that other traffic knows there's a need for caution. Make sure the emergency services are contacted; don't assume this has already been done.

684 Mark *one* answer

You arrive at the scene of a motorcycle crash. The rider is injured. When should their helmet be removed?

- ☐ **A** Only when it's essential
- ☐ **B** Always straight away
- ☐ **C** Only when the motorcyclist asks
- ☐ **D** Always, unless they're in shock

Don't remove a motorcyclist's helmet unless it's essential. Remember they may be suffering from shock. Don't give them anything to eat or drink, but do reassure them confidently.

685 Mark *one* answer

You arrive at an incident. There's no danger from fire or further collisions. What's your first priority when attending to an unconscious motorcyclist?

- ☐ **A** Check whether they're breathing normally
- ☐ **B** Check whether they're bleeding
- ☐ **C** Check whether they have any broken bones
- ☐ **D** Check whether they have any bruising

At the scene of an incident, always be aware of danger from further collisions or fire. The first priority when dealing with an unconscious person is to ensure they're breathing normally. If they're having difficulty breathing, follow the DR ABC code.

686 Mark *one* answer

At an incident, someone is unconscious. What would your priority be?

- ☐ **A** Find out their name
- ☐ **B** Wake them up
- ☐ **C** Make them comfortable
- ☐ **D** Check their airway is open

Remember this procedure by saying DR ABC. This stands for Danger, Response, Airway, Breathing, Circulation. Give whatever first aid you can and stay with the injured person until the emergency services arrive.

687 Mark *one* answer

You've stopped at an incident to give help. What should you do?

- ☐ **A** Keep injured people warm and comfortable
- ☐ **B** Give injured people something to eat
- ☐ **C** Keep injured people on the move by walking them around
- ☐ **D** Give injured people a warm drink

There are a number of things you can do to help, even without expert training. Be aware of further danger from other traffic and fire; make sure the area is safe. People may be in shock. Don't give them anything to eat or drink. Keep them warm and comfortable and reassure them. Don't move injured people unless there's a risk of further danger.

688 Mark *one* answer
There's been a collision. A driver is suffering from shock. What should you do?

- ☐ **A** Give them a drink
- ☐ **B** Reassure them
- ☐ **C** Ask who caused the incident
- ☐ **D** Offer them a cigarette

A casualty suffering from shock may have injuries that aren't immediately obvious. Call the emergency services, then stay with the person in shock, offering reassurance until the experts arrive.

689 Mark *one* answer
You arrive at the scene of a motorcycle crash. No other vehicle is involved. The rider is unconscious and lying in the middle of the road. What's the first thing you should do at the scene?

- ☐ **A** Move the rider out of the road
- ☐ **B** Warn other traffic
- ☐ **C** Clear the road of debris
- ☐ **D** Give the rider reassurance

The motorcyclist is in an extremely vulnerable position, exposed to further danger from traffic. Approaching vehicles need advance warning in order to slow down and safely take avoiding action or stop. Don't put yourself or anyone else at risk. Use the hazard warning lights on your vehicle to alert other road users to the danger.

690 Mark *one* answer
At an incident, a small child isn't breathing. What should you do to try and help?

- ☐ **A** Find their parents and get permission to help
- ☐ **B** Open their airway and begin CPR
- ☐ **C** Put them in the recovery position and slap their back
- ☐ **D** Talk to them confidently until an ambulance arrives

If a young child has stopped breathing, first check that their airway is open and then begin CPR. With a young child, you may only need to use one hand and you shouldn't press down as far as you would with an adult. Continue the procedure until the child is breathing again or until a medical professional takes over.

691 Mark *one* answer
At an incident, a casualty isn't breathing. What should you do while helping them to start breathing again?

- ☐ **A** Put their arms across their chest
- ☐ **B** Shake them firmly
- ☐ **C** Roll them onto their side
- ☐ **D** Tilt their head back gently

It's important to ensure that the airway is open before you start CPR. To open the casualty's airway, place your fingers under their chin and lift it forward.

692 Mark *one* answer
At an incident, someone is suffering from severe burns. What should you do to help them?

- ☐ **A** Apply lotions to the injury
- ☐ **B** Burst any blisters
- ☐ **C** Remove anything sticking to the burns
- ☐ **D** Douse the burns with clean, cool water

Your priority is to cool the burns with clean, cool water. Its coolness will help take the heat out of the burns and relieve the pain. Keep the wound doused for at least 10 minutes. If blisters appear, don't attempt to burst them, as this could lead to infection.

693 Mark *one* answer
You arrive at an incident. A pedestrian is bleeding heavily from a leg wound. The leg isn't broken and there's nothing in the wound. How could you help?

- ☐ **A** Dab the wound to stop the bleeding
- ☐ **B** Keep the casualty's legs flat on the ground
- ☐ **C** Fetch them a warm drink
- ☐ **D** Apply firm pressure over the wound

If there's nothing in the wound, applying firm pressure using a pad of clean cloth or bandage will help stem the bleeding. Don't tie anything tightly round the leg, as this will restrict circulation and could result in long-term injury.

694 Mark *one* answer
At an incident, a casualty is unconscious but breathing. When should you move them?

- ☐ **A** When an ambulance is on its way
- ☐ **B** When bystanders advise you to
- ☐ **C** When there's further danger
- ☐ **D** When bystanders will help you

Don't move a casualty unless there's further danger; for example, from other traffic or fire. They may have unseen or internal injuries. Moving them unnecessarily could cause further injury. Don't remove a motorcyclist's helmet unless it's essential.

695 Mark *one* answer
At an incident, it's important to look after any casualties. What should you do with them when the area is safe?

- ☐ **A** Move them away from the vehicles
- ☐ **B** Ask them how it happened
- ☐ **C** Give them something to eat
- ☐ **D** Keep them where they are

When the area is safe and there's no danger from other traffic or fire, it's better not to move casualties. Moving them may cause further injury.

696 Mark *one* answer

A tanker is involved in a collision. Which sign shows that it's carrying dangerous goods?

☐ A  ☐ B

☐ C  ☐ D

There will be an orange label on the side and rear of the tanker. Look at this carefully and report what it says when you phone the emergency services. Details of hazard warning plates are given in *The Highway Code*.

697 Mark *one* answer

You're involved in a collision. Afterwards, which document may the police ask you to produce?

☐ A Vehicle registration document
☐ B Driving licence
☐ C Theory test certificate
☐ D Vehicle service record

You must stop if you've been involved in a collision which results in injury or damage. The police may ask to see your driving licence and insurance details at the time or later at a police station.

698 Mark *one* answer

After a collision, someone is unconscious in their vehicle. When should you call the emergency services?

☐ A Only as a last resort
☐ B As soon as possible
☐ C After you've woken them up
☐ D After checking for broken bones

It's important to make sure that the emergency services arrive as soon as possible. When a person is unconscious, they could have serious injuries that aren't immediately obvious.

699 Mark *one* answer

A collision has just happened. An injured person is lying in a busy road. What's the first thing you should do to help?

☐ A Treat the person for shock
☐ B Warn other traffic
☐ C Place them in the recovery position
☐ D Make sure the injured person is kept warm

The most immediate danger is further collisions and fire. You could warn other traffic by switching on hazard warning lights, displaying an advance warning triangle or sign (but not on a motorway), or by any other means that doesn't put you or others at risk.

700 Mark *one* answer
At an incident, what should you do with a casualty who has stopped breathing?

- ☐ **A** Keep their head tilted forwards as far as possible
- ☐ **B** Follow the DR ABC code
- ☐ **C** Raise their legs to help with circulation
- ☐ **D** Try to give them something to drink

The DR ABC code has been devised by medical experts to give the best outcome until the emergency services arrive and take care of casualties.

701 Mark *one* answer
You're at the scene of an incident. Someone is suffering from shock. How should you treat them?

- ☐ **A** Reassure them confidently
- ☐ **B** Offer them a cigarette
- ☐ **C** Give them a warm drink
- ☐ **D** Offer them some food

If someone is suffering from shock, try to keep them warm and as comfortable as you can. Don't give them anything to eat or drink but reassure them confidently and try not to leave them alone.

702 Mark *one* answer
There's been a collision. A motorcyclist is lying injured and unconscious. Unless it's essential, why should you not usually attempt to remove their helmet?

- ☐ **A** They might not want you to
- ☐ **B** This could result in more serious injury
- ☐ **C** They'll get too cold if you do this
- ☐ **D** You could scratch the helmet

When someone is injured, any movement that isn't absolutely necessary should be avoided, since it could make the injuries worse. Unless it's essential to remove a motorcyclist's helmet, it's generally safer to leave it in place.

703 Mark *one* answer
What should you do if a trailer you're towing swerves or snakes?

- ☐ **A** Ease off the throttle and reduce your speed
- ☐ **B** Let go of the handlebars and let it correct itself
- ☐ **C** Brake hard and hold the brake on
- ☐ **D** Accelerate until it stabilises itself

Don't be tempted to use harsh braking to stop swerving or snaking, as this could make things worse. You should reduce your speed gradually by easing off the throttle.

704 Mark *one* answer
What should you be aware of when you ride a sidecar outfit for the first time?

- ☐ **A** You need time to get used to it
- ☐ **B** You'll be able to stop in a shorter distance
- ☐ **C** You need to accelerate around bends
- ☐ **D** You can approach corners without braking

A motorcycle with a sidecar, or a trike, will feel very different to ride than a solo motorcycle. It requires a specific technique, especially when cornering, with different methods used for right and left turns. Keep your speed down until you get used to the outfit, especially when negotiating bends and junctions.

705 Mark *one* answer
What may you need to adjust when you're carrying a heavy load on your motorcycle?

- ☐ **A** The footrests
- ☐ **B** The gear lever
- ☐ **C** The seat height
- ☐ **D** The tyre pressure

Carrying extra weight, such as luggage or a pillion passenger, can affect the feel and handling of your motorcycle. If possible, some items may need to be adjusted to help overcome this. These adjustments include the aim of the headlights, the suspension settings, the tyre pressures and the mirrors.

706 Mark *one* answer　　　NI
What are the minimum test vehicle requirements for a motorcycle used to obtain a full category 'A' licence?

- ☐ **A** Solo, with a maximum power of at least 25 kW (33 bhp)
- ☐ **B** Solo, with a maximum power of at least 11 kW (14.6 bhp)
- ☐ **C** Fitted with a sidecar, and with a maximum power of at least 35 kW (46.6 bhp)
- ☐ **D** Solo, with a maximum power of at least 40 kW (53.6 bhp)

To obtain the full category 'A' on your driving licence, the motorcycle you use for your practical test must be a solo machine with a cylinder capacity of at least 595 cc and a power output of at least 40 kW (53.6 bhp).

707 Mark *one* answer

You're carrying a load on your motorcycle's luggage rack. What must you ensure?

☐ **A** The load must be securely fastened
☐ **B** The load must be unevenly balanced
☐ **C** The load must be highly visible
☐ **D** The load must be covered with plastic sheeting

Don't risk losing any luggage while riding: it could fall into the path of following vehicles and cause danger. It's an offence to travel with an insecure load.

708 Mark *one* answer

What does a person need to do when they ride as a pillion passenger?

☐ **A** Have a provisional motorcycle licence
☐ **B** Be lighter than the rider
☐ **C** Wear a motorcycle helmet
☐ **D** Give signals for the rider

Pillion passengers must sit astride the motorcycle, on a proper passenger seat, and passenger footrests must be fitted. They must also wear a correctly fastened motorcycle helmet.

709 Mark *one* answer

What should a pillion passenger do while being carried on a motorcycle?

☐ **A** Give the rider directions
☐ **B** Lean with the rider when going around bends
☐ **C** Take rear observation for the rider
☐ **D** Give arm signals for the rider

When you ride with a pillion passenger, your motorcycle may feel unbalanced and its acceleration and braking distance may also be affected. Make sure your passenger knows they must lean with you while cornering. If they don't, they could cause the motorcycle to become unstable and difficult to control.

710 Mark *one* answer

When you're going around a corner, what should your pillion passenger do?

☐ **A** Give arm signals for you
☐ **B** Check behind for other vehicles
☐ **C** Lean with you on bends
☐ **D** Lean to one side to see ahead

A pillion passenger shouldn't give signals or look around for you – that's your responsibility as the rider. If your passenger has never been on a motorcycle before, make sure they know that they need to lean with you when going around bends.

711 Mark *one* answer
Which of these may need to be adjusted when carrying a pillion passenger?

- ☐ **A** Indicators
- ☐ **B** Exhaust
- ☐ **C** Fairing
- ☐ **D** Headlights

Your headlights must be properly adjusted to avoid dazzling other road users. You'll probably need to do this when carrying a heavy load or the extra weight of a pillion passenger. You may also need to adjust the tyre pressures and the suspension.

712 Mark *one* answer
What's the speed limit on a single carriageway road for a motorcycle towing a trailer?

- ☐ **A** 50 mph
- ☐ **B** 40 mph
- ☐ **C** 60 mph
- ☐ **D** 70 mph

When you tow a trailer, remember that you must obey the reduced speed limits of 50 mph on a single carriageway and 60 mph on a dual carriageway or motorway. Make sure that the trailer is hitched correctly and that any load in the trailer is secure. You should also bear in mind that your stopping distance may increase.

713 Mark *one* answer
What can a heavy load in a motorcycle top box cause?

- ☐ **A** Improved stability
- ☐ **B** Reduced stability
- ☐ **C** Reduced tyre wear
- ☐ **D** Improved braking

Carrying a heavy load in your top box could make your motorcycle unstable, because the weight is high up and at the very back of the machine.

714 Mark *one* answer
Who's responsible for making sure that a motorcycle isn't overloaded?

- ☐ **A** The rider of the motorcycle
- ☐ **B** The owner of the items being carried
- ☐ **C** The licensing authority
- ☐ **D** The owner of the motorcycle

Correct loading is the responsibility of the rider. Overloading a motorcycle can seriously affect the control and handling. It could result in a crash, with serious or even fatal consequences.

715 Mark *one* answer

What should you do before fitting a sidecar to a motorcycle?

☐ **A** Have the wheels balanced
☐ **B** Have the engine tuned
☐ **C** Pass the extended motorcycle test
☐ **D** Check that the motorcycle is suitable

If you want to fit a sidecar to your motorcycle, check that the motorcycle is suitable and can cope with the extra load. Make sure that the sidecar is securely fixed and properly aligned. If your motorcycle was registered on or after 1 August 1981, the sidecar must be fitted on the left-hand side of the motorcycle.

716 Mark *one* answer

You're using throwover saddlebags. Why is it important to make sure they're evenly loaded?

☐ **A** Uneven loads can make the engine overheat
☐ **B** Uneven loads can make the motorcycle uncomfortable
☐ **C** Uneven loads can make the motorcycle unstable
☐ **D** Uneven loads can make the battery overcharge

Panniers or saddlebags should be loaded so that you carry about the same weight in each bag. Uneven loading could make the motorcycle unstable, especially when cornering.

717 Mark *one* answer

You're riding with a bulky tank bag. What could this affect?

☐ **A** Your ability to steer
☐ **B** Your ability to accelerate
☐ **C** Your view ahead
☐ **D** Your insurance premium

If your tank bag is too bulky, it could get in the way of your arms or restrict the movement of the handlebars.

718 Mark *one* answer NI

What requirement must you meet if you want to carry a pillion passenger on your motorcycle?

☐ **A** You must hold a full car licence
☐ **B** You must hold a full motorcycle licence
☐ **C** You must be over the age of 21
☐ **D** You must be over the age of 25

Before you can carry a pillion passenger, the law requires you to have a full licence for the category of motorcycle you're using.

719 Mark *one* answer
When carrying a heavy load on your motorcycle, what may you need to adjust?

☐ **A** Carburettor
☐ **B** Fuel tap
☐ **C** Seating position
☐ **D** Tyre pressures

Take care if you're carrying a heavy load on your motorcycle. Try to carry the weight as low down as possible – ideally in panniers, with the weight evenly spread on each side. You may need to adjust your tyre pressures, your headlight aim and your rear shock-absorber preload setting.

720 Mark *one* answer
You're carrying a pillion passenger. What should you do when you're following other traffic?

☐ **A** Keep to your normal following distance
☐ **B** Get your passenger to keep checking behind
☐ **C** Keep further back than you normally would
☐ **D** Get your passenger to signal for you

The extra weight of a passenger may increase your stopping distance. Allow for this when following another vehicle by increasing the separation distance.

721 Mark *one* answer
When can you carry a child as a pillion passenger?

☐ **A** When they're over 14 years old
☐ **B** When they're over 16 years old
☐ **C** When they can reach the floor from the seat
☐ **D** When they can reach the handholds and footrests

Any passenger you carry – no matter how old they are – must be able to reach the footrests and handholds properly to remain safe on your machine. Also make sure they're wearing protective weatherproof clothing and a properly fitting helmet.

722 Mark *one* answer
What should you check when you fit a sidecar to your motorcycle?

☐ **A** That the sidecar has a registration plate
☐ **B** That the sidecar is correctly aligned
☐ **C** That the sidecar has a waterproof cover
☐ **D** That the sidecar has a spare wheel

If the sidecar isn't correctly aligned with the mounting points, the outfit will be difficult to control and could be dangerous. Riding with a sidecar attached requires a different technique from riding a solo motorcycle. You should keep your speed down while learning this skill.

723 Mark *one* answer
How will riding a motorcycle and sidecar differ from riding a solo motorcycle?

☐ **A** It will allow you to corner more quickly
☐ **B** It will allow you to brake later for hazards
☐ **C** It will require a different riding technique
☐ **D** It will improve your fuel consumption

You'll need to adapt your riding technique when riding a motorcycle fitted with a sidecar. The extra weight will affect the handling and may increase your overall stopping distance.

724 Mark *one* answer
You're carrying a pillion passenger. What should you adjust to allow for the extra weight?

☐ **A** The preload on the front forks
☐ **B** The preload on the rear shock absorber(s)
☐ **C** The balance of the rear wheel
☐ **D** The front and rear wheel alignment

When carrying a passenger or other extra weight, you may need to make adjustments, particularly to the rear shock absorber(s), tyre pressures and headlight alignment. Check your vehicle handbook for details.

725 Mark *one* answer
What's the maximum width allowed for a trailer on a motorcycle?

☐ **A** 0.5 metres (1 foot 8 inches)
☐ **B** 1 metre (3 feet 3 inches)
☐ **C** 1.5 metres (4 feet 11 inches)
☐ **D** 2 metres (6 feet 6 inches)

When you're towing a trailer, you must remember that you may not be able to filter through traffic. Don't forget that the trailer is there, especially when riding round bends and negotiating junctions.

726 Mark *one* answer
What applies when you tow a trailer with your motorcycle?

☐ **A** The motorcycle should be attached to a sidecar
☐ **B** The trailer should weigh more than the motorcycle
☐ **C** The trailer should be fitted with brakes
☐ **D** The trailer shouldn't be more than 1 metre (3 feet 3 inches) wide

To tow a trailer behind a motorcycle, you must have a full motorcycle licence and a motorcycle with an engine larger than 125 cc. Motorcycle trailers mustn't exceed 1 metre (3 feet 3 inches) in width.

727 Mark *one* answer
You have a sidecar fitted to your motorcycle. What effect will it have?

- ☐ **A** It will reduce the motorcycle's stability
- ☐ **B** It will make the steering lighter
- ☐ **C** It will increase the stopping distance
- ☐ **D** It will increase the fuel economy

A sidecar will alter the handling considerably. Give yourself time to adjust to the different characteristics and allow a greater stopping distance.

728 Mark *one* answer
How is a learner motorcyclist's licence restricted?

- ☐ **A** They mustn't carry a pillion passenger
- ☐ **B** They mustn't use the right-hand lane on dual carriageways
- ☐ **C** They mustn't carry panniers on their motorcycle
- ☐ **D** They mustn't ride faster than 30 mph

Learner motorcyclists aren't allowed to
- tow a trailer
- carry a pillion passenger
- use the motorway.
- In addition, they must display red L plates (D plates in Wales) to the front and rear of the motorcycle.

729 Mark *one* answer
What should you do if you want to tow a trailer behind your motorcycle?

- ☐ **A** Display a 'long vehicle' sign on the back of the trailer
- ☐ **B** Fit a larger battery to your motorcycle
- ☐ **C** Hold a full motorcycle licence
- ☐ **D** Use a motorcycle that has shaft drive

You may not ride a motorcycle towing a trailer if you only hold a provisional motorcycle licence.
 When you tow a trailer, you need to be aware that lower speed limits apply and the trailer must be no more than 1 metre wide. The trailer's laden weight should be no more than 150 kg or two-thirds of the kerbside weight of the motorcycle – whichever is less.

730 Mark *one* answer
What should your motorcycle have if you want to carry a pillion passenger?

- ☐ **A** Passenger footrests
- ☐ **B** A passenger communication system
- ☐ **C** A passenger luggage box
- ☐ **D** Passenger grab handles

When carrying a pillion passenger, you should explain to them that they must keep their feet on the footrests. Tell them not to give hand signals, lean away from the rider when cornering, fidget or move around. Also check that they aren't wearing anything long or loose that could get caught in the rear wheel or drive chain.

731 Mark *one* answer
What kind of items should you carry in a top box?

- ☐ **A** Heavy items
- ☐ **B** Personal items
- ☐ **C** Emergency items
- ☐ **D** Lightweight items

Carrying a heavy weight high up and at the very back of the motorcycle can cause problems in maintaining control, particularly when riding at speed. If you have heavy items to carry, it's better to carry them in panniers and keep the weight roughly the same on either side.

732 Mark *one* answer
You hold a provisional motorcycle licence. Are you allowed to carry a pillion passenger?

- ☐ **A** Only if the passenger holds a full licence
- ☐ **B** Not at any time
- ☐ **C** Not unless you're undergoing training
- ☐ **D** Only if the passenger is under 21

You aren't allowed to carry a pillion passenger until you hold a full motorcycle licence. This gives you time to gain riding experience. Even when you've passed your test, don't carry a passenger if you aren't confident that you can do so safely. You're responsible for their safety.

733 Mark *one* answer
What may be seriously affected if you overload your motorcycle?

- ☐ **A** The gearbox
- ☐ **B** The weather protection
- ☐ **C** The handling
- ☐ **D** The battery life

Any load will affect the handling of your motorcycle by changing its centre of gravity. When using panniers, spread the weight evenly on each side. Avoid carrying heavy items in a top box, as this could make your steering dangerously light.

734 Mark *one* answer
You're towing a small trailer on a busy three-lane motorway. What must you do if all the lanes are open?

- ☐ **A** Not exceed 50 mph
- ☐ **B** Not overtake
- ☐ **C** Have a stabiliser fitted
- ☐ **D** Use only the left-hand and centre lanes

The motorway regulations for towing a trailer state that you mustn't
- use the right-hand lane of a three-lane motorway unless directed to do so (for example, at roadworks or due to a lane closure)
- exceed 60 mph.

Glossary

Accelerate

To make the motorcycle move faster.

Advanced stop lines

A marked area on the road at traffic lights, which permits cyclists or buses to wait in front of other traffic.

Adverse weather

Bad weather that makes riding difficult or dangerous.

Alert

A state of mind in which you are quick to notice possible hazards.

Anticipation

Looking out for hazards and taking action before a problem starts.

Anti-lock brakes (ABS)

Brakes that stop the wheels locking so that you are less likely to skid on a slippery road.

Aquaplane

To slide out of control on a waterlogged road surface because a film of water has built up between your tyres and the road, and your tyres are unable to grip the road.

Articulated vehicle

A long vehicle that is divided into two or more sections connected by joints.

Attitude

The way you think or feel, which affects the way you drive. Especially, whether you are patient and polite, or impatient and aggressive.

Awareness

Taking notice of the road and traffic conditions around you at all times when you are riding.

Black ice

An invisible film of ice that forms over the road surface, creating very dangerous riding conditions.

Blind spot

The section of road behind you which you cannot see in your mirrors. You 'cover' your blind spot by looking over your shoulder before moving off, cornering or overtaking.

Brake fade

Loss of power to the brakes when you have been using them for a long time. For example, when riding down a steep hill. The brakes will overheat and not work properly.

Braking distance

The distance you must allow to slow the motorcycle in order to come to a stop.

Brow

The highest point of a hill.

Built-up area

A town, or place with lots of buildings.

Carriageway

One side of a road or motorway. A 'dual carriageway' has two lanes on each side of a central reservation.

Catalytic converter

A piece of equipment fitted in the exhaust system that changes harmful gases into less harmful ones.

Centre stand

An alternative to a side stand, which gives the motorcycle more stability when parked. Also useful for carrying out maintenance checks.

Chicane

A road sign designed to warn road users to slow down because a sharp double bend is coming up on the road ahead.

Choke

Often manual on a motorcycle.

Clearway

A road where no stopping is allowed at any time. The sign for a clearway is a red cross in a red circle on a blue background.

Commentary riding

Talking to yourself about what you see on the road ahead and what action you are going to take – an aid to concentration.

Comprehensive insurance

A motorcycle insurance policy that pays for repairs even if you cause an accident.

Concentration

Keeping all your attention on your riding.

Conditions

How good or bad the road surface is, volume of traffic on the road, and what the weather is like.

Congestion

Heavy traffic that makes it difficult to get to where you want to go.

Consideration

Thinking about other road users and not just yourself. For example, letting another driver go first at a junction, or stopping at a zebra crossing to let pedestrians cross over.

Compulsory Basic Training (CBT)

A one-day training course of predominantly practical training that, when successfully completed, entitles the CBT certificate holder to ride a motorcycle up to 125cc (50cc for 16-year-olds) on the road with 'L' Plates. The certificate is valid for two years but riders are not allowed to carry pillion passengers or ride on motorways.

Contraflow

When traffic on a motorway follows signs to move to the opposite carriageway for a short distance because of roadworks. (During a contraflow, there is traffic driving in both directions on the same side of the motorway.)

Defensive riding

Riding in such a way as to create a safe zone around yourself. Anticipating hazards and the actions of other drivers and keeping yourself safe while riding.

Disqualified

Stopped from doing something (e.g. riding) by law, because you have broken the law.

Distraction

Anything that stops you concentrating on your riding and the other road users around you.

Document

An official paper or card, for example your motorcycle licence.

Drive chain

The chain between the engine and the rear wheel. A poorly adjusted drive chain can cause unpredictable acceleration, fall off or even snap causing injury to the rider or a road accident.

Dual carriageway

One side of a road or motorway, with two lanes on each side of a central reservation.

Engine braking – see also gears

Using the low gears to keep your speed down. For example, when you are riding down a steep hill and you want to stop the motorcycle running away. Using the gears instead of braking will help to prevent brake fade.

Engine cut-out switch

A switch, which is designed to stop the engine in an emergency, for example after a road accident, to prevent fire.

Environment

The world around us and the air we breathe.

Exceed

Go higher than an upper limit.

Exhaust emissions

Gases that come out of the exhaust pipe to form part of the outside air.

Field of vision

How far you can see in front and around you when you are riding.

Filler cap

Provides access to the motorcycle's fuel tank, for filling up with petrol or diesel.

Fog lights

Extra bright rear (and sometimes front) lights which may be switched on in conditions of very poor visibility. You must remember to switch them off when visibility improves, as they can dazzle and distract other road users.

Ford

A place in a stream or river which is shallow enough to ride across with care.

Frustration

Feeling annoyed because you cannot ride as fast as you want to because of other drivers or heavy traffic on the road.

Fuel consumption

The amount of fuel that your motorcycle uses. Different motorcycles have different rates of consumption. Increased fuel consumption means using more fuel. Decreased fuel consumption means using less fuel.

Fuel gauge

A display or dial on the instrument panel that tells you how much fuel (petrol) you have left.

Gantry

An overhead platform like a high narrow bridge that displays electric signs on a motorway.

Gears

Control the speed of the engine in relation to the motorcycle's speed. In a low gear (such as first or second) the engine runs more slowly. In a high gear (such as fourth or fifth), it runs more quickly. Putting the motorcycle into a lower gear as you drive can create the effect of engine braking – forcing the engine to run more slowly.

Handling

How well your motorcycle moves or responds when you steer or brake.

Harass

To ride in away that makes other road users afraid.

Hard shoulder

The single lane to the left of the inside lane on a motorway, which is for emergency use only. You should not ride on the hard shoulder except in an emergency, or when there are signs telling you to use the hard shoulder because of roadworks.

Harsh braking (or harsh acceleration)

Using the brake or accelerator too hard so as to cause wear on the engine.

Hazard warning lights

Flashing amber lights which warn you that a vehicle has broken down. Your hazard warning lights should only be used to warn other traffic that you have broken down. On a motorway you can use them to warn other road users behind of a hazard ahead.

High-sided vehicle

A van or truck with tall sides, or a tall trailer such as a caravan or horse-box, that is at risk of being blown off-course in strong winds.

The Highway Code

Essential reading for everyone, not just learners, *The Highway Code* sets out the rules and regulations for all road-users.

Impatient

Not wanting to wait for pedestrians and other road users.

Indicator

Often referred to as a 'signal' in motorcycling.

Inflate

To blow up – to put air in your tyres until they are at the right pressures.

Instrument panel

The motorcycle's electrical controls and gauges.

Intimidate

To make someone feel afraid.

Involved

Being part of something. For example, being one of the riders in an accident.

Jump leads

A pair of thick electric cables with clips at either end. You use it to charge a flat battery by connecting it to the live battery in another vehicle.

Junction

A place where two or more roads join.

Liability

Being legally responsible.

Lifesaver

Called a 'lifesaver' for good reason, this is the final rearward glance that a rider should give before making any manoeuvre. Forgetting to give a 'lifesaver' could cause you to lose yours.

Manoeuvre

Using the controls to make your motorcycle move in a particular direction. For example cornering or parking.

Maximum

Maximum means greatest so, the 'maximum speed' is the highest speed allowed.

Minimum

The smallest possible.

Mobility

The ability to move around easily.

Monotonous

Boring, for example, a long stretch of motorway with no variety and nothing interesting to see.

MOT

The test that proves your motorcycle is safe to drive. Your MOT certificate is one of the important documents for your motorcycle.

Motorway

A fast road that has two or more lanes on each side and a hard shoulder. Riders must join or leave it on the left, via a motorway junction. Many kinds of slower vehicles – such as bicycles – are not allowed on motorways.

Multiple-choice questions

Questions with several possible options where you have to try to choose the right answer.

Observation

The ability to notice important information, such as hazards developing ahead. The term 'observation' is often used in addition to 'lifesaver'.

Obstruct

To get in the way of another road user.

Octagonal

Having eight sides.

Oil level

The amount of oil that is in the engine. The oil level should be checked as part of your regular maintenance routine, and the oil topped up or replaced as necessary. The engine cannot run effectively and may be damaged if the oil level is too low.

Pedestrian

A person walking.

Pegasus crossing

An unusual kind of crossing. It has a button high up for horse riders to push. (Pegasus was a flying horse in Greek legend.)

Pelican crossing

A crossing with traffic lights that pedestrians can use by pushing a button. Vehicles must give way to pedestrians on the crossing while the amber light is flashing. You must give pedestrians enough time to get to the other side of the road.

Perception

Seeing or noticing (as in Hazard Perception).

Peripheral vision

The area around the edges of your field of vision in which you can see movement but not details. Wearing a motorcycle helmet diminishes a motorcyclist's peripheral vision and means that riders need to use extremely careful observation while riding.

Positive attitude

Being sensible and obeying the law when you ride.

Priority

The vehicle or other road user that is allowed by law to go first is the one that has priority.

Protective clothing

Essential when riding, because it protects the rider from the weather, objects thrown up from the road or in case of an accident.

Provisional licence

A first motorcycle or car licence. All learners must get one before they start having lessons.

Puffin crossing

A type of pedestrian crossing that does not have a flashing amber light phase.

Reaction time

The amount of time it takes you to see a hazard and decide what to do about it.

Red route

You see these in London and some other cities. Double red lines at the edge of the road tell you that you must not stop or park there at any time. Single red lines have notices with times when you must not stop or park. Some red routes have marked bays for either parking or loading at certain times.

Residential areas

Areas of housing where people live. The speed limit is 30mph or sometimes 20mph.

Road hump

A low bump built across the road to slow vehicles down. Also called 'sleeping policemen'.

Road surface

The type and quality of the road that you are riding on. Slippery road surfaces, such as loose chippings, leaves and, even road markings, can make the road surface hazardous for riders, particularly in wet weather.

Rumble strips

Raised strips across the road near a roundabout or junction that change the sound the tyres make on the road surface, warning riders to slow down. They are also used on motorways to separate the main carriageway from the hard shoulder.

Safety margin

The amount of space you need to leave between your motorcycle and the vehicle in front so that you are not in danger of crashing into it if the driver slows down suddenly or stops. Safety margins have to be longer in wet or icy conditions.

Separation distance

The amount of space you need to leave between your motorcycle and the vehicle in front so that you are not in danger of crashing into it if the driver slows down suddenly or stops. The separation distance must be longer in wet or icy conditions.

Shoulder check

A term often used instead of 'lifesaver'.

Side stand

A metal support that enables you to stand your motorcycle when you want, for example, leave it parked. Leaving the side stand down when riding is extremely dangerous and could cause you to have a serious accident, particularly when cornering.

Single carriageway

Generally, a road with one lane in each direction.

Skid

When the tyres fail to grip the surface of the road, the subsequent loss of control of the motorcycle's movement is called a skid. Usually caused by harsh or fierce braking, steering or acceleration.

Slow-riding

Riding a motorcycle in a controlled manner at a walking pace using the throttle, clutch and rear brake.

Snaking

Moving from side to side. This sometimes happens with trailers when they are being towed too fast, or they are not properly loaded.

Staggered junction

Where you drive across another road. Instead of going straight across, you have to go a bit to the right or left.

Steering

Control of the direction of the motorcycle. May be affected by road surface condition and the weather.

Sterile

Clean and free from bacteria.

Stopping distance
The time it takes for you to stop your motorcycle – made up of 'thinking distance' and 'braking distance'.

Tailgating
Riding too closely behind another vehicle – either to harass the driver in front or to help you see in thick fog.

Thinking distance
The time it takes you to notice something and take the right action. You need to add thinking distance to your braking distance to make up your total stopping distance.

Third party insurance
An insurance policy that insures you against any claim by passengers or other persons for damage or injury to their person or property.

Toucan crossing
A type of pedestrian crossing that does not have a flashing amber light phase, and cyclists are allowed to ride across.

Tow
To pull something behind your motorcycle, possibly a small trailer.

Traction Control System (TCS)
A safety system that is fitted to some motorcycles that helps prevent rear-wheel spin on slippery road surfaces.

Traffic-calming measures
Speed humps, chicanes and other devices placed in roads to slow traffic down.

Tram
A public transport vehicle which moves along the streets on fixed rails, usually electrically powered by overhead lines.

Tread depth
The depth of the grooves in a motorcycle's tyres that help them grip the road surface. The grooves must all be at least 1mm deep.

Turbulence
Strong movement of air. For example, when a large vehicle passes a much smaller one.

Two-second rule
In normal riding, the ideal minimum distance between you and the vehicle in front can be timed using the 'two-second' rule. As the vehicle in front passes a fixed object (such as a signpost), say to yourself 'Only a fool breaks the two-second rule'. It takes two seconds to say it. If you have passed the same object before you finish, you are too close – pull back.

Tyre pressures
The amount of air which must be pumped into a tyre in order for it to be correctly inflated.

Vehicle Excise Duty
The tax you pay for your motorcycle so that you may drive it on public roads.

Vehicle Registration Document
A record of details about a vehicle and its owner.

Vehicle watch scheme
A system for identifying vehicles that may have been stolen.

Vulnerable
At risk of harm or injury.

Waiting restrictions
Times when you may not park or load your motorcycle in a particular area.

Wheel alignment
To ensure smooth rotation at all speeds, the wheels of your motorcycle need to be aligned correctly. Poor alignment can cause wheel wobble and make riding and, in particular, cornering dangerous.

Wheel spin
When the motorcycle's wheels spin round out of control with no grip on the road surface.

Zebra crossing
A pedestrian crossing without traffic lights. It has an orange light, and is marked by black and white stripes on the road. Riders must stop for pedestrians to cross.

Answers to questions

Answers to questions

Section 4 – **Safety margins**

146 C	147 D	148 B	149 A	150 A	151 C
152 B	153 D	154 D	155 D	156 C	157 D
158 B	159 A	160 B	161 A	162 A	163 D
164 D	165 D	166 C	167 A	168 C	169 B
170 D	171 B	172 D	173 C	174 D	175 D
176 A	177 B	178 D	179 B	180 D	181 C
182 C	183 B	184 B	185 C	186 A	187 D
188 A					

Section 5 – **Hazard awareness**

189 C	190 C	191 A	192 D	193 C	194 C
195 C	196 D	197 B	198 A	199 A	200 A
201 C	202 C	203 B	204 C	205 D	206 B
207 B	208 C	209 A	210 D	211 D	212 C
213 B	214 C	215 B	216 A	217 A	218 A
219 C	220 A	221 D	222 B	223 C	224 C
225 A	226 A	227 D	228 C	229 B	230 C
231 A	232 D	233 A	234 A	235 D	236 D
237 A	238 C	239 D	240 B		

Section 6 – **Vulnerable road users**

241 D	242 C	243 A	244 A	245 A	246 D
247 B	248 A	249 B	250 A	251 D	252 B
253 C	254 C	255 D	256 D	257 B	258 D
259 D	260 C	261 D	262 D	263 D	264 B
265 D	266 D	267 C	268 C	269 C	270 A
271 D	272 C	273 D	274 D	275 C	276 D
277 A	278 D	279 C	280 C	281 D	282 D
283 B	284 A	285 C	286 C	287 C	288 A
289 D	290 A	291 A	292 B	293 B	294 A
295 A	296 C	297 B	298 D	299 A	300 D
301 D	302 D	303 C	304 B	305 B	306 D

Answers to questions

307 C	308 A	309 A	310 A	311 B	312 B
313 D	314 B	315 B	316 A	317 B	318 B
319 D	320 D	321 A	322 D	323 A	324 A

Section 8 – Vehicle handling

325 A	326 A	327 D	328 D	329 A	330 C
331 C	332 D	333 C	334 D	335 D	336 C
337 C	338 C	339 B	340 B	341 D	342 A
343 B	344 A	345 D	346 B	347 A	348 C
349 D	350 C	351 B	352 C	353 A	354 C
355 C	356 C	357 D	358 D	359 B	360 D
361 A	362 B	363 D	364 A	365 A	366 C
367 B	368 D	369 D	370 C	371 A	372 A
373 A	374 A	375 B	376 D	377 C	

Section 9 – Motorway rules

378 A	379 B	380 A	381 A	382 D	383 C
384 D	385 D	386 D	387 A	388 C	389 C
390 C	391 A	392 C	393 C	394 C	395 C
396 C	397 C	398 B	399 B	400 A	401 B
402 D	403 C	404 A	405 A	406 D	407 B
408 A	409 A	410 C	411 B	412 B	413 D
414 A	415 D	416 D	417 B	418 D	419 D
420 D	421 C	422 A	423 D	424 C	425 B
426 D	427 B	428 D	429 B		

Section 10 – Rules of the road

430 A	431 D	432 B	433 D	434 D	435 D
436 A	437 A	438 D	439 B	440 B	441 C
442 C	443 C	444 D	445 B	446 A	447 C
448 D	449 D	450 A	451 B	452 A	453 B
454 A	455 D	456 A	457 D	458 C	459 A
460 C	461 C	462 B	463 A	464 C	465 A
466 D	467 B	468 A	469 B	470 A	471 B
472 A	473 D	474 A	475 D	476 B	477 C
478 B	479 B	480 B	481 D		

Section 11 – Road and traffic signs

482 C	483 B	484 A	485 D	486 A	487 B
488 A	489 B	490 D	491 D	492 A	493 A
494 B	495 D	496 B	497 D	498 D	499 D
500 A	501 C	502 B	503 D	504 A	505 B
506 B	507 C	508 A	509 C	510 B	511 C
512 D	513 C	514 C	515 D	516 A	517 D
518 D	519 B	520 A	521 A	522 A	523 B
524 B	525 A	526 D	527 A	528 C	529 A
530 B	531 C	532 B	533 D	534 A	535 A
536 C	537 D	538 A	539 C	540 B	541 D
542 B	543 B	544 C	545 C	546 D	547 C
548 B	549 C	550 D	551 B	552 A	553 A
554 C	555 D	556 A	557 C	558 C	559 B
560 A	561 C	562 A	563 A	564 D	565 D
566 B	567 A	568 D	569 C	570 C	571 B
572 C	573 C	574 A	575 B	576 D	577 B
578 B	579 A	580 D	581 A	582 B	583 B
584 D	585 C	586 B	587 C	588 A	589 B
590 A	591 C	592 B	593 B	594 A	595 C
596 A	597 B	598 B	599 B	600 A	601 A
602 B	603 D	604 C	605 B	606 C	607 A
608 C	609 A	610 C	611 B	612 C	613 A
614 B	615 A	616 A	617 D	618 B	619 B
620 B	621 D	622 A	623 B		

Answers to questions

Section 12 – Essential documents

624 A	625 C	626 C	627 B	628 A	629 C
630 D	631 C	632 B	633 A	634 C	635 B
636 D	637 D	638 A	639 C	640 B	641 B
642 C	643 C	644 D	645 D	646 C	647 B
648 B	649 A	650 C	651 A	652 A	653 C
654 D	655 C	656 A	657 A	658 B	659 B

Section 13 – Incidents, accidents and emergencies

660 B	661 A	662 B	663 A	664 B	665 A
666 A	667 D	668 A	669 A	670 C	671 B
672 D	673 B	674 B	675 B	676 D	677 D
678 B	679 A	680 C	681 B	682 D	683 A
684 A	685 A	686 D	687 A	688 B	689 B
690 B	691 D	692 D	693 D	694 C	695 D
696 B	697 B	698 B	699 B	700 B	701 A
702 B					

Section 14 – Motorcycle loading

703 A	704 A	705 D	706 D	707 A	708 C
709 B	710 C	711 D	712 A	713 B	714 A
715 D	716 C	717 A	718 B	719 D	720 C
721 D	722 B	723 C	724 B	725 B	726 D
727 C	728 A	729 C	730 A	731 D	732 B
733 C	734 D				

Personal information

My driver number

Driving instructor's name and
phone number

Driving instructor's number

Theory test date and time

Theory test pass date

Theory test certificate number

Driving school code

Practical test date and time